PORNBURGER

PORNBURGER

HOT BUNS AND JUICY BEEFCAKES

Mathew Ramsey

An Imprint of HarperCollins*Publishers*

HarperCollins books may be purchased for educational, business, or
sales promotional use. For information please e-mail the Special Markets
Department at SPsales@harpercollins.com.

FIRST EDITION

Designed by Ashley Tucker
Photographs copyright ©Matthew Ramsey except:
Martin Swift: comic art
Kate Warren: introduction and acknowledgments
Run Riot Films: Of Fish & Fowl chapter opener
Ashley Tucker: PornBurger Quickie and Porn Stars IRL background photographs

Library of Congress Cataloging-in-Publication Data has been applied for.

ISBN 978-0-06-240865-5

16 17 18 19 20 OV/RRD 10 9 8 7 6 5 4 3 2 1

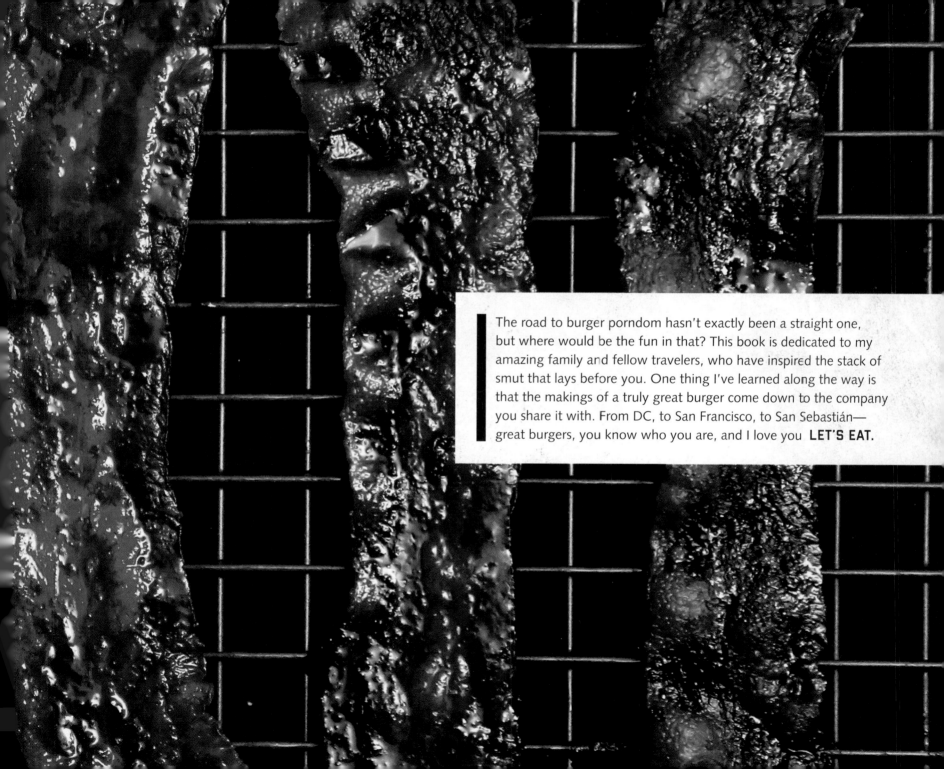

The road to burger porndom hasn't exactly been a straight one, but where would be the fun in that? This book is dedicated to my amazing family and fellow travelers, who have inspired the stack of smut that lays before you. One thing I've learned along the way is that the makings of a truly great burger come down to the company you share it with. From DC, to San Francisco, to San Sebastián— great burgers, you know who you are, and I love you **LET'S EAT.**

Without my journey,
And without the spring,
I would have missed this dawn.

—SHIKI

Your body is not a temple, it's an
amusement park. Enjoy the ride.

—ANTHONY BOURDAIN

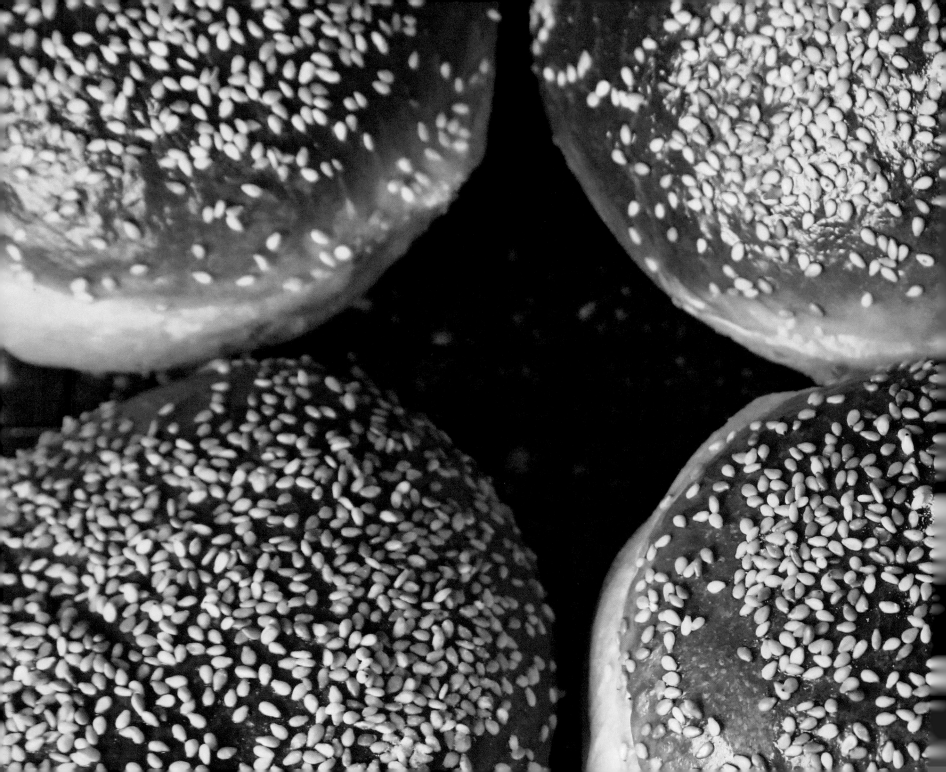

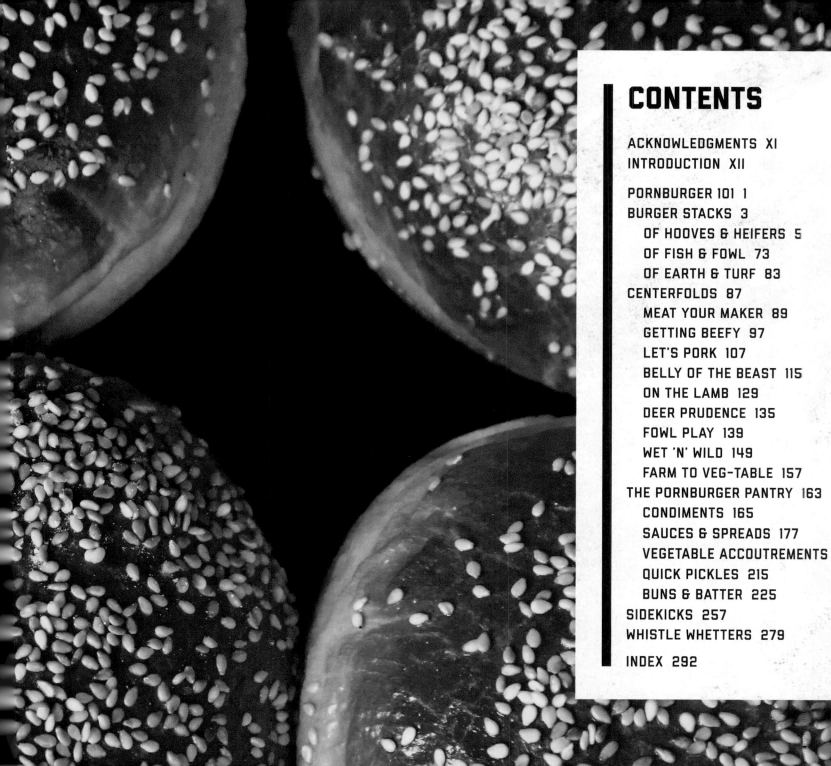

CONTENTS

ACKNOWLEDGMENTS

To Eliot Stein and Julyssa Lopez, for the tacos that started it all. Kate Warren, for your willingness to taste as well as shoot. Martin Swift, for your incredible illustrative talents and late-night conversations. Dave Adams, Josie Swantek, Christ Tuss of Run Riot Productions, for your shared vision, outrageous talent, and Hollywood magic. Kate Nerenberg, for copiloting the Bar R experience and buffing glasses like a champ. Eddie Kim, my cocktail spirit guide. Jason Orfranon, Faturday adventurer and waffle lover. AJ Wilhelm, fellow traveler and late-night wizard. Katie Cleary . . . regards. The rest of my DC family, for your unflinching support. My actual family for . . . well, everything. Loren Reed, my partner and Aussie Hamburglar in crime. Steve Troha and Dado Derviskadic of Folio Literary Management, for e-mailing me a second time and for being rockstar agents. Dan Halpern, Bridget Read, and the incredible team at Ecco Books . . . if I didn't have burger breath, I would kiss you.

INTRODUCTION

We've all been there . . . that singular moment of pure sensory bliss when your toes curl, your eyelids flutter, and you involuntarily release a guttural moan of overwhelming satisfaction and oneness with the universe. Burgers . . . am I right?! Done well, a good burger can leave you wanting both a cigarette and a confessional. But what is it that defines a burger? Is it as simple as the patty? Or is a burger defined by the company it keeps? Buns. Pickles. Onions. Maybe it's more of a feeling. Like love—or smut—you know it when you see it.

Truth be told, I don't have one right answer for you. I just want you on the same page as me—hungry and ready to get weird. Let's be honest: No matter what you tell your family, your friends, or your significant other, you didn't pick this book up "for the articles" and insightful reading. You picked it up because you're a burger pervert, plain and simple. It's OK; I am too. Welcome to the dark side, friend. Welcome to PornBurger.

These aren't your grandparents' burgers, and with a name like PornBurger, they aren't meant to be. Rather, this is an ingredient-driven Choose Your Own Adventure–style experiment, where all roads lead into the mouth of burger madness. If a life of making burgers has taught me anything, it's that burgers come in all shapes and sizes; and a whole world of unique ingredients, recipes, and techniques are just a quick click away. Perfect for the home chef with mad scientist aspirations. In short, the sky is as high as the stack you mack.

This is my burger manifesto for the world at weird. A paint-by-numbers porno, showcasing my much-obsessed-over but never-before-released supply of recipes, along with exclusive sides and beverages to further sweeten the ol' honey pot. But enough of this pussyfooting; let's get filthy.

PORNBURGER 101

There's a certain satisfaction in letting your freak flag fly, especially when that flag is a big, pervy burger. This book was very much written in the spirit of coloring outside the lines. As you work your way through this porn rag, I would encourage you to do the same. Each PornBurger "recipe" contains multitudes of ingredients: Use each "Stack" and accompanying photo as a guide for re-creating my signature monsters, with components listed in order, from toppings through patty, on down to the bun. You'll find instructions for making the individual Stack elements in the back of the book. If amounts for sauces, cheeses, greens, and other toppings seem sketchy, it's because they're up to you—you can stack each Porn-Burger to your fantasy specifications. Feel free to cherry-pick components from the Centerfolds, Pantry, and Sidekicks sections for your own twisted fantasies. Be brazen. Be weird. Man -feast your own destiny!

BURGER STACKS

OF HOOVES & HEIFERS

THE STACK:

SUNFLOWER MICRO GREENS

QUICK PICKLED BEETS (page 216)

1 SLICE PAN-FRIED SPAM

CREAMY HUNTER SAUCE (page 188)

TALEGGIO CHEESE

1 VENISON BURGER (page 136)

1 BRIOCHE BUN (page 226)

I know, I know. With a name like "Bambi" in a book called *PornBurger*, it's easy to make assumptions. Well, I've got three words for you: Slow. Your. Roll. What else would you call a seasoned venison patty smothered in melted Taleggio cheese, creamy *sauce chasseur* ("hunter sauce"), quick pickled beets, and pan-fried Spam and sandwiched in a buttery bun?

THE BAMBI

BAO-SER'S CASTLE BURGER

THE STACK:

SEARED SLOW-ROASTED PORK BELLY (page 116)

CILANTRO

RICE VINEGAR CUCUMBER PICKLES (page 216)

SLICED GREEN ONIONS

1 SEARED ONION-SOUP-BRAISED BEEF TONGUE PATTY (page 100)

HOISIN MAYONNAISE (page 168)

1 STEAMED BAO BUN*

*Available at your local Asian grocery store

These White Castle–inspired beauties take as much inspiration from the Midwest as they do from the Far East. Bao chicka fucking wow wow.

THE STACK:

PORNBURGER SMOKY BURGER SAUCE (page 166)

GRILLED RED ONIONS

SLICED TOMATO

1 JUICY FLOOZY PATTY (page 101)

A FEW SLICES OF CRISP-COOKED APPLEWOOD-SMOKED BACON

JALAPEÑO PICKLES (page 219)

SHREDDED ROMAINE LETTUCE

1 SESAME BRIOCHE BUN (page 227)

What does this burger have to do with Bill Murray? Absolutely nothing. Well, unless of course you're Bill Murray. In that case, this is a very personal public invitation to join me for a burger and a beer. Also, I'm pretty sure this is what he whispered into Scarlett Johansson's ear at the end of *Lost in Translation*. This looker with a heart of gold is seared on the outside, medium-rare on the inside, with a molten core of melted cheese and a creamy sous-vide egg yolk. Stack this fatty with shredded lettuce, bacon, quick pickled jalapeño, tomato, and my smoky burger sauce, and you too may become a Bill-iever.

SOUS-VIDE COOKING

The term *sous-vide* (French for "under vacuum") is an intimidating concept for your average at-home cook. How does it work? What does it do? How do I pronounce this without sounding like an idiot?

In layman's terms, sous-vide (pronounced sue-VEED) is a method of cooking in which food is sealed airtight in a plastic bag and then submerged in a hot water bath, where it's cooked at a constant temperature. The "hot water bath" can be anything from a stockpot to a Cambro container, simply filled with water. The contraption that actually heats and maintains the water temperature is what's called an immersion circulator. This tool allows you to precision-cook food to a certain temperature without overcooking, while maintaining all of its moisture and nutrients. Translation: the perfect pork chop . . . the perfect steak . . . the perfect burger.

GORDY'S PICKLE JAR, DC

WWW.GORDYSPICKLEJAR.COM

There are a lot of ways to measure success. As a fanboy of Sarah Gordon and Sheila Fain's handcrafted pickles, I personally measure it by the first time I received a complimentary jar of their Cajun Okra. They're that good.

When it comes to pickles in the District, Gordy's are the absolute standard. From farmers' markets to just about every fast-casual, they're everywhere, and with good reason. Local produce, responsibly sourced spices, and subtle sophistication are at the very heart of their operation.

PRO TIP:

FOR LIFE-CHANGING PICKLEBACK SHOTS,
TRY THEIR THAI BASIL JALAPEÑO BRINE.

THE STACK:

BALSAMIC GLAZE*

FRESHLY SHAVED BLACK TRUFFLE

TRUFFLE WHIPPED GOAT CHEESE (page 185)

FOIE GRAS MOUSSE (page 185)

KALAMATA OLIVE/ONION CONFIT AND CHERRY CAKE (page 249)

2 PORNBURGERS (page 91)

A FEW SLICES OF CRISP-COOKED BACON

PORT WINE ONION JAM (page 181)

*Commonly available in the vinegar section at your grocery store

This beefcake is soooooo good-looking, my friend Jeremih went and wrote a song about it. Now you can have your burg-day cake and eat it too. This savory Kalamata olive, cherry, and caramelized onion cake comes layered with creamy foie gras mousse, smash-cooked beef patties, a few slices of bacon, onion jam, and truffle whipped goat cheese. Go ahead, blow out your candles and make a wish . . . I'll wait.

CALICORNICATION

THE STACK:

ROASTED TOMATILLO SALSA (page 188)

ANCHO-CHILE-RUBBED GRILLED CORN (page 194)

PORK RINDS

QUESO FRESCO

CHORIZO HOLLANDAISE (page 189)

1 SOUS-VIDE POACHED EGG (page 143)

1 PORNBURGER (page 91)

SLICED AVOCADO

1 ENGLISH MUFFIN

This burger is some serious hard-core soft-corn porn. Riding raunchy on top of an English muffin sits a smutty beef patty adorned with a poached egg, chorizo hollandaise, grilled ancho-rubbed corn, and some salty pork rind crumble for texture. Dream of Cali-corn-ication.

THE STACK:

QUICK PICKLED HAMBURGER DILLS (page 216)

SMOKED SHIITAKE "BACON" (page 212)

CARAMELIZED ONIONS (page 199)

SLICED SWISS CHEESE

1 PORNBURGER (page 91)

KIMCHI THOUSAND ISLAND DRESSING (page 168)

2 ROOT VEGETABLE LATKES (page 254)

Chanukah may have already come and gone, but this stoner stack is the gift that keeps on giving: smoky shiitake mushrooms on a nest of caramelized onions, kimchi Thousand Island dressing, a seared beef patty draped in a slice of melted Swiss, and a couple of crispy root vegetable latkes, or as I call them—Chanukah hash. Light 'er up!

THE CHRONIC-KAH BURGER

CREAMED PORN

THE STACK:

MUSTARD GREEN AIOLI (page 168)

PEA SPROUTS

PICKLED OKRA

1 COLD-SMOKED TOMATO (page 207)

CREAMED CORN (page 204)

SLICED CHEDDAR CHEESE

1 PORNBURGER (page 91)

1 SESAME BRIOCHE BUN (page 227)

I should probably start off by saying that I LOVE me some creamed corn porn. Fresh out of the skillet, fresh out of the can, whatever. This Southern-sullied sexploit brings out the sinner in me. I'm talking a PornBurger beef patty topped with a slice of cheddar, creamed corn, a cold-smoked tomato, pickled okra, crispy pea shoots . . . AND a mustard green aioli to boot. Sure, this beauty is well endowed, but since when is size an issue? I read somewhere that it's all about the motion in the ocean . . . whatever that means.

THE STACK:

FRESHLY GRATED NUTMEG

PARMESAN MORNAY (page 187)

1 FRIED DUCK EGG (page 143)

COUNTRY HAM

2 SMASH-COOKED PORNBURGERS (page 91)

SLICED APPLEWOOD-SMOKED GRUYÈRE CHEESE

DIJON MUSTARD (page 172)

1 LIÈGE WAFFLE (page 234)

This Belgian stack of martial artistry is a real uppergut punch to your average brunch. Beefy in all the right places, this knife-and-forker comes stacked with a Belgian Liège waffle, a spoonful of Dijon mustard, two smash-cooked patties, a slice of applewood-smoked Gruyère, a slice of country ham, an over-easy duck egg, AND Parmesan Mornay for days. Your move, team Chuck Norris.

THE STACK:

CHEESE CURDS*

BONE MARROW POUTINE SAUCE (page 264)

BLACK GARLIC* FRIES (page 264)

1 PORNBURGER (page 91)

QUICK PICKLED HAMBURGER DILLS (page 216)

SHREDDED MUSTARD GREENS

BROWN KETCHUP (page 173)

1 ONION ROLL, SPLIT AND GRILLED

*Available online

This juicy stack of smut rides a high horse and wears a mighty hat. We're talking aboot a juicy PornBurger patty loaded with black garlic potatoes fried in beef leaf fat, smothered in a rich bone marrow poutine sauce, and topped with cheese curds. In the words of the great Akinyele, "Just poutine in my mouth."

THE STACK:

MESCLUN GREENS

RED ONION PICKLES (page 219)

SLOW-ROASTED LAMB BELLY (page 132) **SLATHERED IN STRAWBERRY HARISSA** (page 180)

FRESH GOAT CHEESE

1 PORNBURGER (page 91)

SLICED HEIRLOOM TOMATO

TARRAGON GREEN GODDESS DRESSING (page 170)

1 TOASTED BRIOCHE BUN (page 226)

This sultry stack of seduction is curvy in all the right places. Slow-roasted lamb belly slathered in strawberry harissa offers a lingering kiss of sweet heat, balanced by a spoonful of cool tarragon green goddess dressing and a schmear of fresh goat cheese. In other words, this mature beauty is a real "s-lamb dunk."

HARISSA TOMEI

HORN DOG

THE STACK:

CLOVER HONEY

WHOLE KERNEL CORN/JALAPEÑO BATTER (page 255)

SLOW-ROASTED PORK BELLY (page 116)

SEARED PICKLED HOT DOG (page 220)

2 SMASH-COOKED PORNBURGERS (page 91)

There's no reason hot dogs should have all the fun. This boner of a burger builds off the American classic and achieves new heights with a cut of pickled beef frank and a slice of crispy pork belly sandwiched between two smash-cooked beef patties, dipped in a jalapeño/corn batter, fried whole, AND drizzled with honey (see the batter recipe for assembly and frying instructions). Because . . . meat on a stick.

THE STACK:

CHEESEBURGER POP TART PASTRY (page 228)

CHEESEBURGER POP TART FILLING (page 228):
BACON JAM, BEEF, SHALLOTS, HAMBURGER DILLS, CHEESE

PORNBURGER SMOKY BURGER SAUCE (page 166)

This after-school special is a meme-nto of my childhood: beef patty, with a bacon onion jam and melty American cheese, stuffed inside buttery pop tart pastry, with burger sauce for dipping. (Assemble and bake the pop tart as described on page 228.)

CHEESEBURGER POP TART

THE INGLORIOUS BASQUERED

THE STACK:

CANDIED JAMÓN (page 119)

SEARED FOIE GRAS (page 140)

1 OXTAIL BURGER WITH SWEET VERMOUTH OXTAIL JUS (page 104)

ROASTED PHYSALIS SHALLOT COMPOTE (page 178)

RUSTIC COUNTRY BREAD

Bueno. This Basque beauty is a pinch sweet, a pintxo salty, and all kinds of Spanish lisp-y. Behold, this braised oxtail burger comes served in its own sweet-vermouth-fortified jus, topped with seared foie gras and candied jamón Ibérico, and skewered to a crispy slice of rustic white bread lathered in a roasted physalis shallot compote. San Sebastián . . . you complete me.

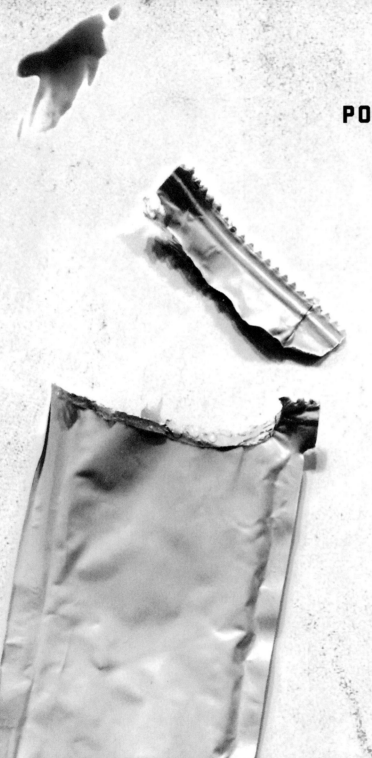

SAN SEBASTIÁN

I'm not exactly what you'd call a religious man, but I do believe there's a heaven on Earth. A Garden of Feedin' if you will (oof, sorry about that one) in San Sebastián, Spain. This Basque Country culinary destination is so studded with Michelin stars, you can probably see it from space. On top of that, almost every bar doubles down as a pintxos (pronounced "peenchos") pusher. Think cured meats, seafood, pimentos, and all sorts of naughty combos skewered on a stick and served with bread, and your choice of beaches on which to sleep it all off.

PRO TIP: The sign of a good pintxos bar can be measured by the number of discarded paper napkins on the floor. Contrary to what you may think, the more, the merrier.

MEATS & FOODS, DC

247 FLORIDA AVENUE NW, WASHINGTON, DC 20001
WWW.MEATSANDFOODS.COM

This intimate six-seater, aptly named Meats & Foods, is without a doubt the best sausage party in town. Food baby of Ana Marin and Scott McIntosh, Meats & Foods is unpretentious, simple, and consistently special. Their sausages reflect the notion of doing one thing and doing it well—really, really well. Signature sausages served up from this humble hole in the wall include DC's darling half-smoke (with perfect snap), a beautifully milky brat, and a brilliantly balanced Italian you can have served hot, or take home to throw on your own grill. Sausages are made fresh daily, and choice vegetable sides come locally sourced from nearby farms and sometimes even neighbors.

THE STACK:

QUICK PICKLED BEETS (page 216)

TRUFFLED DEMI-GLACE (page 186)

GRUYÈRE DE COMTÉ CHEESE*

1 PORNBURGER (page 91)

BONE MARROW ONION JAM (page 182)

POTATO-CHIP-CRUSTED FOIE GRAS GOUGÈRE (page 237)

*Available at a fancy cheese store or online

This bromantic stack of sophistication has three degrees and a black belt in French kissing. We're talking a slice of melted Gruyère de Comté over a beef patty, a black truffled demi-glace, bone marrow onion jam, a gratuitous dick joke, pickled beets, and an oven-crisped cheese puff. In fact, the only thing missing from this beastie is a shirtless Seth Rogen.

THE JAMES FRANCOPHILE

THE STACK:

SEARED FOIE GRAS (page 140)

BACON PEANUT BUTTER (page 182)

1 PORNBURGER (page 91)

PORT WINE ONION JAM (page 181)

POTATO-CHIP-CRUSTED FOIE GRAS GOUGÈRE (page 237)

At first blush, it's easy to assume this barely legal slider seduction is just another hot piece of PB&J. Well, let's just say the devil's in the details. This petite package is composed of potato-chip-encrusted foie gras pâte à choux, a smear of sultry sweet onion jam, a heaping spoon of bacon peanut butter, pan-seared foie gras, and a beef patty. Foie real you ask? Foie 100 percent serious.

THE STACK:

RADISH AND PURPLE BASIL MICRO GREENS

PINEAPPLE GASTRIQUE (page 188)

1 CHICKEN-FRIED PIG EAR (page 270)

1 COMPRESSED WATERMELON PATTY (page 158)

RICE VINEGAR CUCUMBER PICKLES (page 216)

GOAT CHEESE

1 GOAT CHEESE BEIGNET (page 242)

This bright beauty rocks out with its melons out. Stacked with simple sophistication, this burger balances the sweetness of compressed watermelon and a goat cheese beignet with the savory seduction of chicken-fried pig ear, and the sultry tartness of a pineapple gastrique. Go on, take a picture. It'll last longer.

MELON MONROE

THE STACK:

THINLY SLICED RADISH

CAPERS

PICKLED FENNEL (page 220)

UNI BEURRE BLANC (page 190)

1 PORNBURGER (page 91) **SEASONED WITH FURIKAKE** *

SEAWEED SALAD *

2 SHRIMP TOASTS (page 246)

*Available at any local Asian or Japanese market,
in the Asian section of your grocery store, or online

This mythical beast of a burger is all muscle splendor on top and hot tail on bottom. Nesting on crunchy shrimp toast and a bed of seaweed salad sits a juicy furikake-seasoned burger, bathed in a sea urchin beurre blanc and adorned with a spoon of capers, pickled fennel, and thinly sliced fresh radishes. This is one merman comfortable being equal parts surf and turf.

THE STACK:

1 RAW QUAIL EGG YOLK

TROUT ROE

BEET CHIPS

1 STEAK TARTARE PATTY (page 103)

ANCHOVY AIOLI (page 168)

GRILLED SOURDOUGH BREAD

I might be biased, but I'm pretty sure burgers are an aphrodisiac. Then again, what do I know? For me, sexy food is adventurous, exotic, raw, and flavor vibrant. This seasoned beef tartare, with an ocean-fresh anchovy aioli, a handful of earthy beet and purple potato chips (which you can find in your grocery or health food store), raw creamy quail yolk, and a spoonful of trout roe, meets all of the above credentials. Cupid might be an "ass man," but I aim for the heart.

MY BLOODY VALENTINE

THE PICKLEBACK

PORKNADO

THE STACK:

IPA CHEDDAR CHEESE SAUCE (page 187)

BEER-BRAISED PORK CHEEKS (page 126)

1 DOUBLE-FRIED PICKLE "PATTY" (page 160)

RED CABBAGE SLAW (page 219)

1 PRETZEL ROLL

What does a phallus patty of pickled goodness have to do with whiskey anyway? Turns out, the answer is "everything." If you aren't already familiar with the Pickleback, you're only hurting yourself. The concept is simple: a shot of whiskey, followed by a shot of pickle juice. For this burger, I've changed the game but kept the rules the same. A shot of whiskey (see Note), followed by a mouthful of fried pickle, spicy cabbage slaw, beer-braised pork cheek, and naughty cheddar-beer sauce. Hold on to your butts.

NOTE: Traditionally Old Crow or Jameson is used for Picklebacks, but feel free to mix it up.

THE STACK:

CILANTRO AND BABY ARUGULA SALAD (DRESSED WITH RICE VINEGAR)

CARAMELIZED ONIONS (page 199)

CRISP-COOKED DUCK BACON WITH PUMPK'N SPICE BACON RUB (page 123)

PUMPKIN AIOLI (page 170)

1 COFFEE-RUBBED PORNBURGER (page 91)

SLICED TOMATO

1 BRIOCHE BUN (page 226)

This pumpkin plumper (plumpkin?) comes in only one size: extra grande. With a coffee-rubbed beef patty slathered in a pumpkin aioli, caramelized onions, a few slices of pumpkin-spiced duck bacon, tomato, and a bright herb salad, this stack-o'-lantern is surely a smug smiley.

PUMPKIN SPICE FATTE

PORKNADO

THE STACK:

RED CABBAGE SLAW (page 219)

CARNITAS (page 125)

AVOCADO CREMA (page 178)

1 PRIMO PORK BURGER (page 108)

GRILLED PINEAPPLE BUTTER (page 178)

1 ENGLISH MUFFIN, SPLIT AND TOASTED

This burger might just be the perfect storm. A pork sausage patty with whipped avocado crema, crispy ancho-rubbed carnitas, red cabbage slaw, and a slightly smoky grilled pineapple butter make this lil' piggy a true force of nature.

THE STACK:

SLICED GREEN ONIONS

TRUFFLED SAUSAGE GRAVY (page 190)

1 FRIED EGG

CRISPY HASH BROWN NEST

SLICED OR GRATED EXTRA-SHARP CHEDDAR CHEESE

1 PORNBURGER (page 91)

1 CHEDDAR BUTTERMILK BISCUIT (page 233)

Breakfast for dinner? Fuck that. This is breakfast for winner. Be advised: Periods of prolonged staring could lead to potential heart failure and/or unruly beard growth. Please consult with your family physician before consuming this brawny biscuit burger. That said, there are certainly worse ways to go than "death by burger."

THE SLUMBERJACK

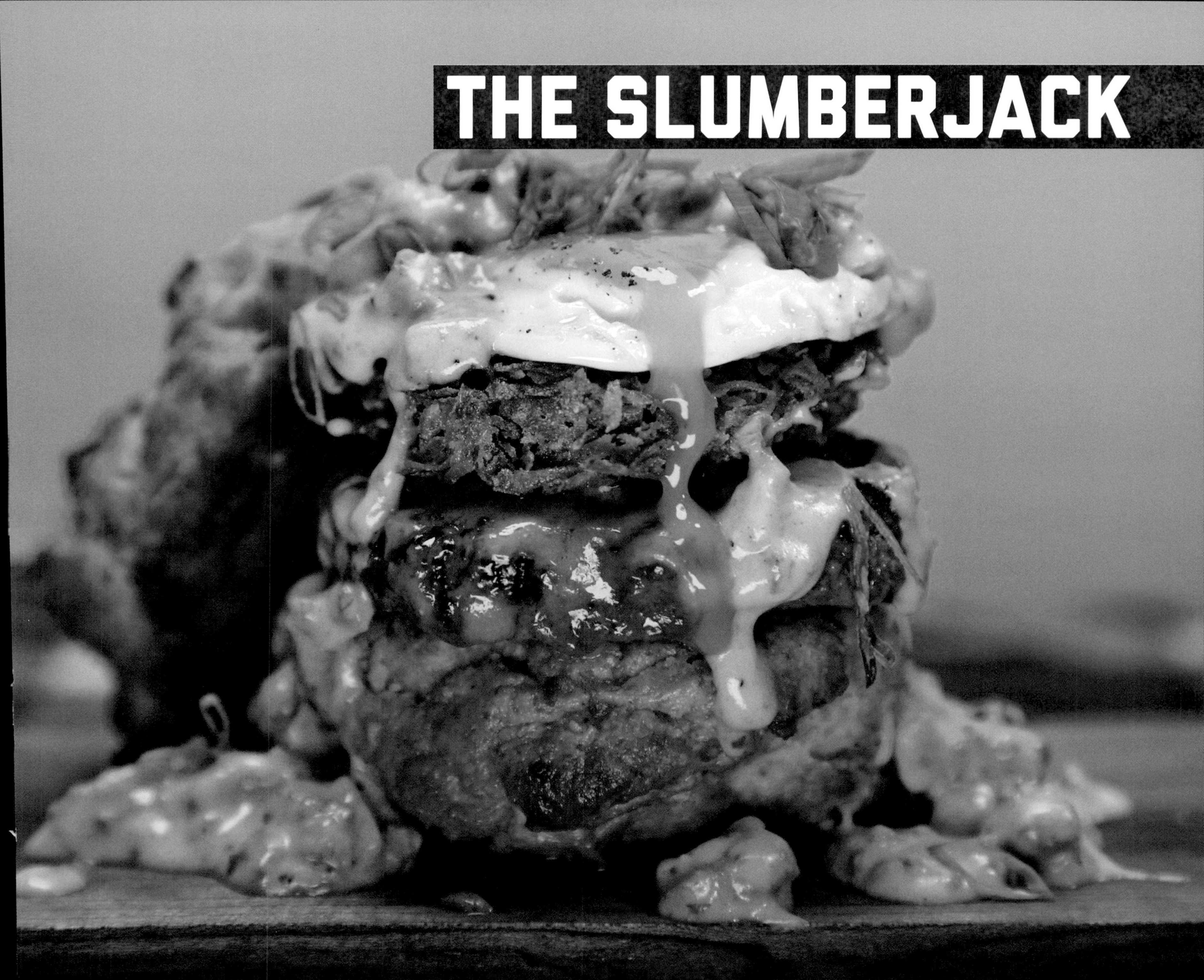

SO KALBI MAYBE

THE STACK:

KIMCHI TEMPURA (page 274)

SLICED GREEN ONIONS

1 FRIED EGG

1 PORNBURGER (page 91) **SEASONED WITH GOCHUJANG***

CILANTRO

1 RICE BUN (page 238)

*Available at any local Asian market, in the
Asian section of your grocery store, or online

Hey, I just met you. And this is crazy—but here are my grilled rice cakes, with a gochujang-slathered PornBurger patty, a fried egg, a few sprigs of cilantro, and a spicy kimchi tempura. So kalbi maybe.

THE STACK:

PINEAPPLE UPSIDE-DOWN CAKE (page 250)

CRISP-COOKED BACON WITH JALAPEÑO BACON RUB (page 123)

RIESLING CHEDDAR CHEESE SAUCE (page 187)

1 PORNBURGER (page 91)

CRISPY "SPAM FRIES" (page 120)

This perky beach blonde classic is stacked with all kinds of salty and sweet, and is not afraid to flaunt it. Sandwiched between a split sun-kissed pineapple upside-down cake sits a beef patty, pan-fried Spam, crispy jalapeño-rubbed bacon, and a gorgeous sharp cheddar Riesling sauce.

THE SPREAD-EAGLE BURGER

THE STACK:

MUMBO SAUCE (page 174)

1 BEER-BATTERED "FRENCH FRY" BUN

DICED ONIONS

PICKLE RELISH

SLICED AGED WHITE CHEDDAR CHEESE

1 HALF-SMOKE BURGER STUFFED WITH BEEF CHEEK CHILI (page 111)

What's more 'merica than a burger crafted from its capital's very own culinary traditions? This District denizen bleeds red, white, blue, and beef cheek chili. With a patty constructed from my half-smoke-inspired grind, Gordy's pickle relish, a slice of aged white cheddar, and a French fry bun, drizzled in mumbo sauce—America, this star-spangled beaut is for you.

THE STACK:

KIMCHI KETCHUP (page 174)

CRISP-COOKED BACON WITH WHITE MISO PARMESAN BACON RUB (page 123)

BLACK-VINEGAR-MARINATED ONIONS (page 200)

1 PORNBURGER (page 91)

QUICK PICKLED HAMBURGER DILLS (page 216)

BLACK GARLIC AIOLI (page 168)

1 BRIOCHE BUN (page 226)

There's umami . . . and then there's UMILFY. This savory bombshell of sensuality knows exactly how to get those juices flowing. Sandwiched in a squishy brioche bun, lathered in kimchi ketchup and a black garlic aioli, this cougar comes stacked with a PornBurger beef patty, sautéed onions marinated in black vinegar, and white miso Parmesan bacon. Helllllo, Mrs. Robinson!

THE UMILFY

OM(S)G!!!

It's hard to talk about our beloved savory sensation, umami, without talking about its falsely vilified crystalline cousin, monosodium glutamate (MSG). What we know as umami is simply the taste imparted by the amino acid glutamate and ribonucleotides in certain delicious foods like, for example, burgers. These proteins and ribonucleotides are found in every single living thing and occur naturally in everything from Parmesan cheese, to beef, to tomatoes. So how is MSG different? It's not. MSG is simply the glutamate that has been isolated, most commonly from fermented sugar beet or sugarcane molasses. Think of it like taking a vitamin C pill instead of eating an orange. And while some people might actually be allergic to MSG, chances are that you're not. MSG is as safe and natural to eat as table salt. There is no science to support thinking that MSG is harmful in the amounts we eat it.

ECOFRIENDLY FOODS, VA

There's a good chance you've already heard of EcoFriendly Foods co-founder and farmstar Bev Eggleston. He's been featured in just about every food publication there is, and his sustainably raised, fatty pork has been championed up and down the East Coast by such culinary giants as Momofuku, Gramercy Tavern, and even Chipotle. A farmer first, Bev is disrupting business as usual, with a model that focuses on food integrity. He offers artisanal, certified humane farms "the opportunity to sell their finished animals—live—to EcoFriendly Foods for a premium price, who then handle the rest of the process: slaughter, processing, marketing, distribution, and receivables." Not surprisingly, the result is hog heaven on earth. Want to meet the legend? Bev can often be found rocking out with his hog out at the Dupont Circle farmers' market.

THE STACK:

CAFFEINATED MAPLE SYRUP (page 189)

2 APPLE FRITTER DOUGHNUTS

SLICED SHARP CHEDDAR CHEESE

1 MAPLE-BACON-WRAPPED BURGER (page 98)

If you're anything like me, you start your weekends extremely high (. . . on life), and extremely hungry. This morning glory combines all of my breakfast binging necessities—something sweet, something savory, caffeine—and a WHOLE lot of bacon. Sandwiched between two warm and freshly glazed apple fritter doughnuts sits a maple-bacon-wrapped beef patty, draped with slices of melty cheddar cheese, and drizzled with a caffeinated maple-espresso syrup. Munchie devils begone!

THE STACK:

CRISPY ASPARAGUS SHAVINGS (page 198)

SPRING PEA KETCHUP (page 174)

GRILLED FETA CHEESE

1 LAMB BURGER (page 130)

LEMON AND RADISH SLICES

CILANTRO AND MINT SALAD (DRESSED WITH EXTRA-VIRGIN OLIVE OIL AND CIDER VINEGAR)

RUSTIC SOURDOUGH BREAD

This spring beastie is a real Jean-Claude Van Lamb kick to the face. Bright notes of lemon and garlic battle it out with a robustly seasoned lamb patty, grilled feta, and crispy asparagus, making this burger a mammoth dressed in sheep's clothing.

THE WOOLY LAMB-OTH

THE WILLEM DAFOE-NUT

THE STACK:

CORNICHON RELISH (page 180)

FRENCH ONION DIP

CRISP-COOKED BACON WITH BLACK PEPPER

1 SMASH-COOKED PORNBURGER (page 91)

1 DEESNUT (page 241)

This American badass with French roots delivers an intensely layered performance on a buttery Parmesan crescent roll doughnut with French onion dip, cornichon relish, and black peppered bacon. What do you think . . . Dafriend or Dafoe?

THE STACK:

SHOESTRING ONION RINGS (page 277)

MUSTARD CAVIAR (page 172)

POTATO PARSNIP GRATIN (page 211)

1 LAMB BURGER (page 130) **DRIZZLED WITH DEMI-GLACE** (page 186)

YORKSHIRE PUDDING (page 253)

This Yorkshire pudonk-a-donk has got some serious junk in its trunk. Know what I mean? Stuffed inside a deliciously golden Yorkshire pudding sits a succulent lamb beastie, sauced with a rich demi-glace, and crowned with a potato and parsnip gratin, crispy shoestring onion rings, and mustard caviar. Stay calm and burger on.

THE YORKSHIRE PUDD-TANG

OF FISH & FOWL

THE STACK:

FRESHLY SHAVED SUMMER TRUFFLE

FOIE GRAS COGNAC SAUCE (page 185)

1 DUCK BURGER AU POIVRE (page 142)

SUNFLOWER AND BEET MICROGREENS

SLICED HEIRLOOM TOMATO

1 BRIOCHE BUN (page 226)

This summer sexpot has all its ducks in a row: pan-fried duck breast, encrusted in a smattering of peppercorns, smothered in a foie gras cognac cream sauce, and feathered with shaved summer truffle, a nest of greens, and a slice of tomato. In other words . . . this burger is straight-up quack cocaine.

A FISH CALLED HITACHI WANDA

THE STACK:

CHERRY PEPPER SPREAD (from Gordy's; see page 13)

OLD BAY AND BACON POTATO SALAD (page 208)

1 SMOKED TROUT BURGER (page 153)

WATERCRESS

1 OLIVE OIL BUN

This stack of self-gratification could make a nun weak in the knees. A lightly fried smoked trout burger dressed in an Old Bay–seasoned bacon potato salad and a spicy dollop of Gordy's cherry pepper spread is enough to make even Harry Potter jealous of this wand(a).

THE STACK:

SRIRACHA MUSTARD (page 172)

ARUGULA

CRISP-COOKED SMOKED BACON

AMERICAN CHEESE

1 FRIED CHICKEN THIGH (page 146)

QUICK PICKLED HAMBURGER DILLS (page 216)

1 WHITE CASTLE CHEESEBURGER WAFFLE (page 230)

No really, I did. And then I got right back in bed, fell asleep, and did it all over again. Crispy fried chicken, White Castle cheeseburger waffles, bacon, dill pickles, and a spicy Sriracha mustard elevate these chicken 'n' waffles to their very best. All morning I be flossin' on that, flawless.

THE STACK:

1 FRIED MACARONI AND CHEESE BUN (page 245)

CRISP-COOKED BACON WITH JERK BACON RUB (page 123)

1 LOBSTER BURGER (page 150)

SLICED TOMATO

PURPLE KALE

I'm going to let this burger perversion speak for itself: fried macaroni and cheese buns, jerk-rubbed bacon, lobster . . . mic drop.

OF EARTH & TURF

THE STACK:

TRUFFLE BALSAMIC GLAZE*

FRESH AND ROASTED BRUSSELS SPROUTS (page 197)

SHALLOT CONFIT (page 203)

1 VEGGIE BURGER (page 159)

BLACK GARLIC AIOLI (page 168)

1 KALAMATA OLIVE BUN

*Available from your local grocer or online

Ian MacKaye–inspired, this hard-core burger is TOTES straight (v)edge. With a crispy beet and chickpea patty, crunchy Brussels sprouts, shallot confit, and black garlic aioli, this red and black stack of umami angst is certain to strike veggie dis-chord in the hearts of the burger mainstream.

FUGAZIM

CENTERFOLDS

MEAT
YOUR
MAKER

ON PATTIES: A PROVOCATION

Here's where we get our hands dirty in the art of patty provocation (think Patrick Swayze and Demi Moore in *Ghost*). I realize that not everybody is going to have the time OR mechanics to grind their own burger blend, but in this section I'm going to discuss why you might just want to start. Let's be honest: If you're reading this book, it's probably because you're trying to step up your burger game, and grinding your own burger blend is the easiest way to level up.

WHERE TO BEGIN

First things first—step away from the processed, prepackaged ground beef. Most often when you're purchasing packaged ground beef at your local supermarket, you're picking up a collection of ground beef scraps. I know, I know—the label reads "ground sirloin." What that basically means is the majority (at least 50 percent) of the meat is sirloin. The fact that it's a collective mix of meat doesn't make it inherently bad. It simply means that your purveyor is practicing the art of "head to tail," or no waste. However, we still don't know exactly what's in the blend, and for the sake of our mission—to create THE BEST BURGER EVER—we're aiming for full-on flavor control.

On top of that, there's a good chance your processed ground beef was run through a chemical wash AND injected with a preservative, to stretch shelf life and give the appearance of prepackaged freshness. Again, this is not necessarily a bad thing, but I think it's safe to say we're not looking for the *appearance* of freshness—we want the real deal. So why not scooch a little closer to the actual source?

The laws of common sense and of cooking in general dictate that what you put into something is basically what you get out of it.

In other words, the quality of your burger is going to have a direct correlation to the quality of ingredients that compose it. Start out with quality beef, and you're giving yourself an undeniable advantage. Aim for "prime" or "high choice" cuts. These are the highest graded qualities, and have the most marbling.

GOING BUTCH

I suggest you make nice with your local butcher—you know, that intimidating person behind the counter with the big cleaver? Don't be nervous: A good butcher will be more than happy to indulge you in any of your meaty questions. After all, this is what they do. Butchers aren't in it for the money. They're in it for the craft, which means they take an immense sense of pride in what they do, the quality of meat they sell, and the knowledge they can share. Ask the right questions, and you'll be getting the best cuts because they want you to come back. I usually start with a simple icebreaker like, "Do you know if this sexy heifer was more of a Taurus or a Scorpio?" Then I follow up with the heavy hitters like, "Where was the cow raised?" "What was its diet?" "What breed is it?" "Is the beef hormone free?" "Was it dry-aged?" And, most important, "If this cow was on Tinder, would you right or left swipe?"

GRASS-FED VS. GRAIN-FED

Here's a little secret: All cows are grass fed for the majority of their lives. It's how they spend the final 15 percent of their days that is actually up for debate, and there are enough meat politics at play to make your head spin.

Environmentally speaking, the answer depends on whom you ask and where the cattle are being raised. It's important to understand that both grass- and grain-finished cattle can come at a hefty environmental cost. Commercial feedlots are notorious environmental offenders, but grass-fed cattle aren't exactly exempt. Pasture-raised cattle actually take more time to get to weight (about eight extra months), which makes them less efficient and can dramatically impact their environmental footprint.

From a health perspective, grass-fed beef is easy to tout as being better for you. It's leaner, chock-full of omega-3 fatty acids, and more likely to be hormone free. However, there are some studies that state that grain-fed cattle, finished on a diet of primarily corn and sorghum, actually have higher amounts of omega-9 fatty acids than their grass-fed counterparts, and are lower in total saturated and trans fats. What the what?!

In my opinion, if you're looking to burgers as a means of healthy living, you're doing it wrong. Flavor is in the fat, which in turn translates to marbling. You'll find marbling in grass-fed beef, but not nearly as much as in grain-finished. Grass-fed beef tends to be a little chewier, with grassy and sour flavor notes.

Bottom line, the best way to buy your beef responsibly is to know where your meat comes from and how it's raised. There's a good chance your smaller, local farm is doing something right. (Cue: butcher bestie high five!)

DRY-AGED BEEF

When it comes to buying cuts of beef, I can be a bit of an ageist. Read: age over beauty. When beef gets dry-aged in a controlled environment, it undergoes several enzymatic and bacterial processes that lead to a maturation in flavor, as well as tenderization. The entry point for dry-ageing is 14 days, but it can go all the way up to 120! The longer the beef ages, the more intense and concentrated the flavors get (as well as the price tag). With regard to burgers, I like to grind in some aged sirloin (28 to 45 days) to punch up that beefy burger steez. If you want to follow suit, make sure to the remove the outer crust before grinding, to prevent contaminating your blend with naturally occurring pathogens and bacteria.

THE PORNBURGER BLEND

After lots of tinkering and experimenting in the kitchen, I've landed on what I consider the perfect beef blend, using just three cuts. It's a well-rounded burger with plenty of fat that balances notes of buttery richness, nuttiness, and even a subtle kiss of grass. Without further ado . . .

THE PORNBURGER BLEND:
  1 part sirloin (preferably aged)
1½ parts short rib
  2 parts chuck

DAT GRIND

OK, so you're Facebook friends with your butcher, and you've got your gorgeous, prime cuts of local, dry-aged beef Instagram-ed. What's next?

Slice those beautiful cuts into long strips roughly 1 inch wide, arrange them on a baking sheet, cover, and place in your freezer. Keep the different cuts separate, for the time being, as there's a good chance your butcher gave you more than needed to fulfill the recipe ratio. The goal is to firm up your beef so that when you grind it, the meat will maintain some of its shape integrity. Warm meat has a tendency to compact, and compacted meat will throw off your texture endgame, as well as juiciness. Toss your grinder parts (grinder, blades, dyes) in the freezer too. Twenty to 30 minutes ought to do the trick.

When your meat has chilled the fuck out, it's time to assemble your grinder and prepare for some of that sweet, sweet nasty—or in the words of Pharrell, "Grindin'."

I personally use the KitchenAid grinder attachment to fulfill the majority of my grindhouse needs. It comes with two grinder dyes/plates, a large one (⅜ inch) and a smaller one (¼ inch). For that melt-in-your-mouth texture, we'll actually use both.

To start, grind each cut separately through the larger dye. Grind it on a low speed to prevent the meat from getting overworked. There's a good chance you'll have leftovers of each cut, so it's important to weigh everything after this grind, because we're looking for a pretty exact ratio. What to do with the extra ground beef? I save mine for either meatloaf or a killer Bolognese sauce.

Once everything has been weighed out, go ahead and use your mitts to mix everything together, making sure to evenly distribute all that beautiful fat. Depending on how much time has elapsed, you might want to throw the meat back in the freezer to cool again. Remember, texture is a HUGE part of the experience.

With all of the cuts integrated, it's time for that grind once again. This time, grind the collective through the smaller plate. Make sure the ground beef stays loose as it collects. Meat, don't compact on me now!

When everything is ground, form your patties with a light touch (see Getting in Shape, at the top of the next column) and refrigerate. Cooking with cold patties will ensure a more evenly cooked burger. Also, refrain from seasoning the patties at this point. Salt will only start to cure the beef, making it tough before you even cook it.

Don't have a KitchenAid? Hand-crank grinders can be bought on the Interwebs on the cheap. Plus, they look cool. If your butcher's not crazy busy, you can ask him to grind the cuts separately, but I wouldn't count on that. If you're really invested, you can simply mince all your meat by hand. However, the best texture is still going to be ground.

GETTING IN SHAPE

Do these patties make my buns look big? When it comes to shaping your patties, there are some important things to consider. Namely, what kind of construct are you looking for? A slider? A double smash-cooked burger? A bigger bistro burger? No matter the answer, you're going to want, and need, a digital scale. This will ensure that all of your patties both cook and look the same. Here are my size recommendations:

SLIDER: 2.5 ounces
SMASH-COOKED BURGER: 4 ounces
BISTRO BURGER: 6 ounces

Once you've weighed and portioned out your patties, use cupped hands to VERY loosely form each portion into a ball. They should almost be falling apart. From there, gently press that meat into patty submission. (But leave the meat in a ball if you're going to be making a smash-cooked burger; see Smash-Cooked Burger, page 94.) Refrigerate the patties until ready to cook.

Note: Overworking and compacting the meat will only lead to a denser, drier patty, so just like wearing clothes, less is more.

IT'S GETTING HOT IN HERE

There are a million ways to skin a cat, and even more ways to cook a burger. Let's talk basics.

SIX DEGREES OF DONENESS

Cooking to the proper degree of doneness is literally as easy as reading a thermometer. Measure the temperature from the center of the burger, and simply cook to the first number in the range.

Once they've been removed from the heat, allow the burgers to rest for about 5 minutes. While they're resting, the residual heat will continue to cook your burgers an additional 5 degrees or so.

RARE: 120°–125°F
MEDIUM-RARE: 125°–130°F
MEDIUM: 130°–135°F
MEDIUM-WELL: 135°–140°F
WELL DONE: 140°–145°F
SEVEN YEARS OF BAD SEX: 145°–160°F*

The United States Department of Agriculture recommends 160°F for ground meat (to ensure that all areas of the food have reached a temperature of 140°F or higher). Eat at your own risk.

SMASH-COOKED BURGER

Surrender yourself to the "smash." This process is all about introducing as much meaty surface area to a hot pan as possible. The result? A flavor-enhancing crispy, crusted exterior (à la the Maillard reaction) with a perfectly juicy interior. While this process might seem to fly in the face of everything you know about making a juicy burger, the patty is smashed before its fat has had a chance to render, and the result is sublime. Don't believe me? Take it from my friend Shake Shack.

For the perfect smash burger, preheat a sturdy cast-iron pan or griddle over medium-high heat with a little oil. When the oil is close to smoking, season your chilled ball of ground beef liberally with salt and pepper, and place it in the pan.

Using a sturdy metal spatula, immediately smash that baby down with as much pressure as you can muster. Let that patty cook until it's crispy and browned—about 1½ minutes should do the trick. Using that same spatula, scrape the patty up in one fast, hard

movement, making sure to get all of that crust we just worked so hard to achieve, and flip. This is when you would add the cheese, if that's your thing. These patties cook quickly, so another 30 seconds is about all you need to finish. Scrape the patty up again and allow it to rest before serving.

SKILLET/PAN-FRIED

Without a doubt, this is my favorite way to prepare a bistro-style burger. Similar to the smash process, this method cooks the patty in its own flavorful juices. To begin, preheat your cast-iron pan over medium-high heat, with a dab of butter and a splash of oil—you don't need much, just enough to lubricate the pan. If you want to get all fancy-pants, you can also add some aromatics, like a couple of smashed garlic cloves and a couple of sprigs of thyme. When the pan is hot and ready to sear, liberally season both sides of your chilled patty with salt and pepper and place it in the pan. Unlike with the smash patty, we're going to flip the fuck out of this mound of meat. Somewhere along the way, the unsubstantiated fear of flipping was instilled deep within our souls. Many today argue for the "one and done" methodology. This is empirically false. Flipping on repeat actually shortens cook time, achieves just as much browning, AND makes for a more evenly cooked burger. So for flip's sake, rotate that burger roughly every 45 seconds, until you get to your desired level of doneness. Add cheese when you're close to temp. Once that patty has reached your happy place, remove it from the heat and allow to rest.

GRILL

I love me a good flame-licked patty. There's something about cooking meat over an open fire that induces the most primal of involuntary erections. For starters, make sure your grill grate is clean and thoroughly scraped down. For gas grills, preheat over high heat at least 15 minutes before cooking. For charcoal grills, make sure the coals are glowing orange and ashed over. When you're ready to cook, brush each patty with canola oil, make a slight indent in the top with your finger to ensure that it cooks flat, and season liberally with salt and pepper. Place the patties on the grill and cook away. Much like the skillet version, feel free to flip that patty on the reg, until you achieve your desired level of doneness. Do not under any circumstances "squish" that burger, or you'll lose your precious fat, flavor, and all sense of dignity. Add cheese when you're close to temp, remove from the grill, and allow to rest.

SOUS-VIDE

Burgering la sous-vide-a loca is a super-simple way to gently cook your meat to temp, while sealing in all those wonderful flavors and juices. And while this method takes longer than the others, the time spent is pretty hands off, and the result is a perfectly pasteurized, medium-rare burger with a crispy finish. So if you're nervous about undercooked meat but harbor a carnal craving for red meat, this burger is for you.

To begin, set your sous-vide water bath to 131°F using the immersion circulator. Once the water has come to temperature, place the patties in zip-top plastic bags, one per bag, but don't close the bags yet. Using what's called the water displacement method, you're going to slowly dip each bag in the water, allowing the water to push out the air from the bag. Zip-seal the bag when almost all the air has been displaced. We do this instead of vacuum sealing to avoid compacting the patties. Cook in the water bath for 1 hour.

Preheat your cast-iron pan or griddle. Remove the burgers from the bags, season liberally with salt and pepper, and sear. Because the patties have already been cooked to temperature, this part goes super quick, 30 to 40 secs per side. Remove from the heat and allow to rest.

GETTING BEEFY

MAPLE-BACON-WRAPPED BURGERS

When I set out to make these behemoths, I had one goal: to get crispy bacon on the outside and perfectly cooked medium burgers on the inside. After nothing short of 24 hours of tinkering I arrived at the following two-part cooking method, which involves frying to crisp the bacon and finishing in the oven. While it may sound like a bit of a hassle, the result is worth the effort. ▪ **MAKES 4 BURGERS**

1 Preheat the oven to 375°F. In a deep fryer or a deep heavy-bottomed pan with at least 2 inches of oil, preheat your fry oil to 350°F. While the fry oil and oven come to temp, construct your patties. We're essentially going to make a bacon lattice to drape over the formed patties. Begin with 2 slices of bacon, placed side by side and vertically aligned. Next, "weave" in 2 horizontally aligned slices, alternating over and under placement. Trim roughly an inch off of each bacon end to prevent excessive overlap when we wrap the patties. (Excess bacon . . . I know it sounds silly. Save the bacon scraps for other purposes.) Place the patty on top of the lattice and season with salt and pepper. Wrap the bacon tightly around the patty so that the bacon just slightly overlaps on top. Fasten the bacon slices with one or two toothpicks. Repeat this process for the remaining patties.

2 Carefully drop the patties into the hot oil and fry until the bacon begins to brown and is slightly crispy, about 5 minutes. Drain the patties on paper towels and then immediately place on a baking sheet. Lightly sprinkle the bacon with brown sugar, and finish the burgers in the oven for 10 minutes, or until they reach a desired level of doneness. (Mind your thermometer!) If you want to drape these dudes in cheese, top them with a slice when the burgers are about 5 degrees from your goal. Remember, the patties will generally rise an additional 5 degrees as they rest, so really that's 10 degrees. Don't forget to remove the toothpicks before serving!

Vegetable oil, for deep-frying
Four 6-ounce PornBurger patties (page 91)
16 slices maple bacon (about 1 pound)
Kosher salt and black pepper
¼ cup brown sugar, for sprinkling
4 slices extra-sharp cheddar cheese (optional)

ONION-SOUP-BRAISED BEEF TONGUE PATTIES

For some people, the very idea of eating tongue can be hard to swallow. Something about French-kissing their food . . . prudes. Done well, beef tongue is one of the cow's sexiest muscles—tender on the inside, seared crispy on the outside, and punch-drunk with beefy flavor brawn. ▪ **MAKES 8 TO 12 SERVINGS**

1 Run the tongue under cold water to rinse. Transfer the tongue to a large pot and add the beef stock, onions, celery, garlic, bay leaf, sugar, salt, and peppercorns. Bring the pot to a gentle simmer, cover, and cook for 3 hours. The tongue is done when the outer layer of skin is easily removed and the meat is fork-tender. If it's not done after 3 hours, simmer for another 30 minutes. Allow the tongue to cool slightly on a cutting board until you can handle it with your bare mitts. Peel off all of the outer skin and remove any extraneous fat. Slice the tongue horizontally into ⅓-inch-thick slabs and then cut into slider-size squares, roughly 2 x 2 inches.

2 Preheat a cast-iron pan with a drizzle of olive oil over medium-high heat. Cook each cut of tongue for about 1 minute on each side, or until you get a good sear. Season the tongue with salt and pepper, and serve immediately.

3 pounds fresh beef tongue
2 quarts beef stock
4 onions, sliced
2 stalks celery, roughly chopped
2 cloves garlic, peeled
1 bay leaf
1 tablespoon sugar
1 tablespoon kosher salt, plus more for seasoning
1 teaspoon black peppercorns
Extra-virgin olive oil, for searing
Black pepper

THE JUICY FLUUZY PATTIES

These patties utilize science to build off of the shoulders of St. Louis giant, the Juicy Lucy, by adding some creamy yolk-popp'n persuasion to the equation. For those of you not keeping score, each floozy is one sous-vide-cooked beef patty, one sous-vide-cooked egg yolk, and a whole lot of melty cheese. ▪ **MAKES 4 PATTIES**

1 Use your thumbs to press a sizable divot in the center of each of the formed patties and press a cheese round onto each one. Carefully crack open your sous-vide eggs and gently remove the whites. Place a cooked yolk on half of the patties. Gently cover each yolked patty with an unyolked patty. Wet a finger or two and run along the seam of the two patties to make into one glorious patty. Be mindful not to squeeze down on the center, so as not to break the yolk.

2 Set your sous-vide water bath to 131°F using your immersion circulator. Place the patties in zip-top plastic bags, one per bag, and use the water displacement method (see page 95) to push out the air from the bag. Zip-seal the bags and place in the water bath to cook for 1 hour.

3 Preheat a skillet or griddle over medium-high heat and drizzle it with oil. Season the patties liberally with salt and pepper and sear them on each side for about 1 minute, or until crispy. Serve immediately.

Eight 4-ounce PornBurger patties (page 91)

8 slices American cheese, cut into 2-inch rounds (I use my ¼-cup measure as a cutter)

4 extra-large eggs,* cooked sous-vide for 45 minutes at 148°F (see page 143)

Extra-virgin olive oil, for the pan

Kosher salt and black pepper

*I usually make a couple extra, just in case of breakage.

STEAK TARTARE PATTIES

Ooh, baby, I like it raw. For this recipe, make sure you're sourcing your beef from a reputable place. It also doesn't hurt to mention to your butcher that you will be preparing tartare, so he gives you the best cut. After all, you'll be serving the beef in its most vulnerable, unadulterated state. ▪ **MAKES 4 PATTIES**

1 Before you slice and dice up that nice piece of tenderloin, throw it in the freezer for at least 30 minutes. You don't want to freeze it completely, but you want to get it firm enough that you can make clean cuts. Cut the beef into a small dice and refrigerate until ready to serve.

2 When you're ready to plate, combine the tenderloin, shallot, fried garlic, capers, thyme, parsley, avocado oil, vinegar, mustard caviar, sesame oil, Worcestershire sauce, and chili flakes in a medium bowl. Use a spatula to fold together. Season to taste with salt and pepper.

3 To serve, use a 3-inch circle mold to stack the tartare patties. Garnish each with a quail egg yolk, 1 teaspoon trout roe, and beet chips. Serve immediately as is or with toasted sourdough slathered in my anchovy aioli.

* Available at your local Asian market or online

** You can often find these at an organic grocery store or at your local Asian market. Or you can use a chicken egg. In either case, make sure you're using either pasteurized or very fresh eggs from a reputable source. Ya dig?

*** Straight-up potato chips also work well.

14 ounces beef tenderloin

1 shallot, minced

1 tablespoon fried garlic*

2 teaspoons capers, drained and roughly chopped

1 teaspoon minced fresh thyme

2 teaspoons minced fresh flat-leaf parsley

1 tablespoon avocado oil or fruity olive oil

2 teaspoons black vinegar

2 teaspoons Mustard Caviar (page 172)

1 teaspoon sesame oil

1 teaspoon Worcestershire sauce

½ teaspoon chili flakes

Kosher salt and black pepper

4 quail egg yolks**

4 teaspoons trout roe (optional), for garnish

Beet chips*** (optional), for garnish

OXTAIL BURGERS WITH SWEET VERMOUTH OXTAIL JUS

While traditionally, oxtail was just that—the tail of an ox—today the cut most commonly refers to the tail of a cow. Oxtail is a perfect example of a rags-to-riches story. Coaxed through the braising process, oxtail transforms from an inexpensive, bony piece of meat to a truly rich and succulent cut, full of flavor. ▪ **MAKES 4 BURGERS**

1 Melt the butter in a large cast-iron pan over medium heat. Add the onions, carrot, celery, and garlic and sweat.

2 While the vegetables are sautéing, combine 1 cup flour, 1 teaspoon salt, and 1 teaspoon pepper in a bowl. Lightly dredge the oxtail in the flour mixture and add the oxtail to the vegetables. Brown the oxtail on all sides. Pour in the absinthe and very carefully flambé. Let the fire burn out before adding the red wine, beef stock, sweet vermouth, bay leaf, thyme, parsley, and sugar. Cover and gently simmer for 3 hours.

3 Once the oxtail is tender, remove the meat from the braising liquid and allow it to cool. Reserve the braising liquid; we're going use it to pour over the burger.

4 In the meantime, in a deep fryer or a deep heavy-bottomed pan with at least 2 inches of oil, preheat your fry oil to 325°F. Using an immersion blender, puree the braising liquid and reduce the sauce over medium-high heat until it has the consistency of a gravy, about 20 minutes. Season to taste with salt and pepper. Cover the jus and keep it warm until ready to serve.

5 Once the oxtail has cooled to a manageable temperature, use your fingers to debone and shred the meat. You'll find the shredded meat molds easily. Shape the shredded oxtail into compact patties for frying. In a small bowl, combine the remaining flour, salt, and pepper. Dredge the patties in the flour mixture and fry for about 5 minutes, or until crispy on the outside. When you're ready to plate, finish the oxtail patties with a healthy drizzle of jus.

2 tablespoons butter
2 onions, chopped
1 carrot, chopped
3 stalks celery
2 cloves garlic
2 cups all-purpose flour
2 teaspoons kosher salt
2 teaspoons black pepper
2¼ pounds oxtail
¼ cup absinthe
2 cups red wine
1 quart beef stock
1 cup sweet vermouth
1 bay leaf
6 sprigs thyme
6 sprigs parsley
3 teaspoons sugar
Kosher salt and black pepper
Vegetable oil, for frying

LET'S
PORK

PRIMO PORK BURGERS

The secret to making killer pork burgers is in the grind. Preground meat is fine, but because it's usually packed down tight when it's wrapped, you are starting out of the gate at a serious disadvantage. A densely packed patty is going to yield a densely cooked patty, simple as that. The fix is easy: Give preground pork a quick pass through your grinder at home. Adding bacon fat never hurts either. The result: pure patty seduction. ▪ **MAKES 4 BURGERS**

1 Mix the pork, bacon, shallot, garlic, cilantro, chili flakes, and allspice together in a bowl so that everything is fully integrated. Run the mix through your grinder, making sure to keep the grind loose. Carefully measure out the patties on a scale so that they're about 4½ ounces each. Form the patties as lightly and with as little pressure as possible, to ensure the ideal consistency. The less you handle them, the better.

2 Preheat a cast-iron pan over medium-high heat, with a drizzle of olive oil. Cook the patties for about 3 minutes on each side. You want them just cooked through, but not hockey pucks.

1 pound ground pork shoulder, chilled

4 slices black forest bacon, minced and chilled

1 shallot, finely minced

1 clove garlic, finely minced

1 tablespoon fresh cilantro, minced (or sage if you want a more breakfast-style burger)

1 teaspoon chili flakes

A pinch of ground allspice

Extra-virgin olive oil, for the pan

HALF-SMOKE BURGERS STUFFED WITH BEEF CHEEK CHILI

This is my personal riff on a DC standard. Rather than actually smoke the patties, I use bacon in the grind to impart some of those smoky notes, and beef cheek in my chili because I love the braiser-sharp flavor that the tender cut offers. Imagine all the beefiness of a *Magic Mike* dance routine whittled down to a single hip thrust, and you'll be on the same page. ▪ **MAKES 5 STUFFED BURGERS**

1 Mix the pork, beef, bacon, all the spices, the sugar, onion powder, garlic powder, mustard powder, salt, and pepper together in a bowl so that everything is fully integrated. Run the mix through your grinder, making sure to keep the grind loose. Carefully measure out the patties on a scale so that you have 4 patties that are 4 ounces each and 4 that are 2 ounces each. These are the tops and bottoms of the stuffed patties.

2 Form the larger bottom patties and, using your thumb, make a sizable indent in the top, to form a cup. For the tops, lightly roll them into a ball and flatten to a slightly wider diameter than that of the indent in your bottom patties. Ladle a heaping tablespoon of chili into the dent you made in each of the bottom patties, and cover with the top patties. Crimp the patties together to seal. If it helps, I also dip my fingers in water and run along the edges to seal.

1 pound pork shoulder, ground

1 pound chuck, ground

4 slices smoked bacon, ground

1½ teaspoons coriander seeds, toasted and ground

¾ teaspoon cumin seeds, toasted and ground

1½ teaspoons smoked sweet paprika

½ teaspoon cayenne pepper

½ teaspoon ground mace

¼ teaspoon ground turmeric

1½ teaspoons sugar

2¼ teaspoons onion powder

RECIPE CONTINUES ▶▶

3 Preheat a cast-iron pan over medium-high heat, with the oil. Gently cook the patties for about 3 minutes on each side, or until nicely browned.

1¼ teaspoons garlic powder
1¼ teaspoons mustard powder
1½ teaspoons kosher salt
½ teaspoon black pepper
⅓ cup Beef Cheek Chili (recipe follows)
1 tablespoon extra-virgin olive oil

BEEF CHEEK CHILI
MAKES 1 QUART

1 As with all other meat cuts, it helps to have the beef cheeks slightly frozen before slicing; 20 minutes in the freezer ought to do it. Roughly chop each cheek into bite-size cubes (about ½-inch chunks).

2 Preheat an extra-large cast-iron or heavy-bottomed pot with the vegetable oil over high heat.

3 Toss the chopped cheeks in the flour and pat off any excess. Liberally season the cheeks with salt and black pepper. Add to the pan and brown until crispy on each side. We're not trying to cook the cheeks through, just adding a nice crust that will enhance the beef flavor. Once the cheeks have been nicely browned, remove the meat from the pan, keeping the oil, and allow to rest. Depending on the size of your pan, you might have to do this step in two stages.

4 In the same pot, sauté the onion over medium heat, until translucent. Add a little oil to the pan if necessary, but do so sparingly. Toss in the garlic and jalapeño, and cook until fragrant. Return the beef to the pan along with the tomato paste, beef broth, cumin, chili powder, sugar, chipotle powder, and bay leaf and bring to a boil. When everything is bubbling, bring the pot down to a gentle simmer. Cover the pot with foil and gently braise, stirring occasionally, until tender and flavorful, approximately 3 hours. Season to taste with salt and pepper. To serve the chili stuffed in a burger, allow the chili to cool completely first. This can be made a day ahead of time for better flavors and to help with overall timing.

2 pounds beef cheek, trimmed, sinew removed
3 tablespoons vegetable oil, plus more as needed
½ cup all-purpose flour
Kosher salt and black pepper
1 onion, diced
2 medium cloves garlic, minced
1 jalapeño, diced
⅓ cup tomato paste
2 cups beef broth
1½ teaspoons cumin
3 tablespoons chili powder
2 tablespoons plus 1 teaspoon sugar
1 tablespoon chipotle powder
1 bay leaf

PORNBURGER QUICKIE:

HALF-SMOKES

Ask any District denizen about the indigenous food of DC, and every single one of them will mention the half-smoke, DC's signature street meat with a presidential seal of approval to boot. I can say this with confidence for two reasons. (1) Half-smokes are THAT good, and (2) the laundry list of indigenous DC foods is rather short (like, I can only think of one other thing short). Made famous by the legendary Ben's Chili Bowl (home of the OG chili half-smoke), half-smokes can be found at street carts, butchers, and bars alike.

So what is a half-smoke? Well, it depends on whom you ask. To some, it's an oversize beef frankfurter that has been "half smoked" (whatever that means). For others, it's a coarse-ground sausage of half pork, half beef with a hint of spice and a lot of snap. And for others still, it's simply a smoked sausage that's been split and smoosh-fried. And you know what? They would all be right. There are A LOT of variations of this District darling, but my absolute favorite comes from the sausage whisperers over at Meats & Foods (see page 35) in Bloomingdale, so treat yo'self.

PRO TIP: When ordering your half-smoke, ask for it with chili, onions, and mustard.

BELLY
OF THE
BEAST

SLOW-ROASTED PORK BELLY

Seared pork belly always makes me blush. This recipe is super hands off and yields perfect belly every time. It should be noted that as it roasts, a dark crust will form on the outside of the belly. Have no fear; it's all a part of the flavor experience. ▪ **MAKES 8 TO 16 SERVINGS**

1 Combine the brown sugar, salt, and pepper in a small bowl. Rub the mixture all over the pork belly, place in a sealable container, and refrigerate overnight.

2 Preheat the oven to 450°F.

3 Remove the pork belly from the fridge and discard any liquid. Place the belly, fat side up, on a rimmed baking sheet and cook for 1 hour.

4 Remove the belly from the oven and brush with any accumulated juices. Drop the oven temperature down to 250°F and continue to cook for 2 more hours, brushing with juices periodically. Remove the belly from the oven and allow to cool. For clean-cut pieces, wrap the cooled belly in plastic wrap and refrigerate before slicing into ¼-inch pieces.

5 To serve, sear each side in a skillet over medium-high heat, about 2 minutes per side.

¼ cup packed light brown sugar
2 tablespoons kosher salt
1 teaspoon black pepper
2 pounds pork belly, skin removed

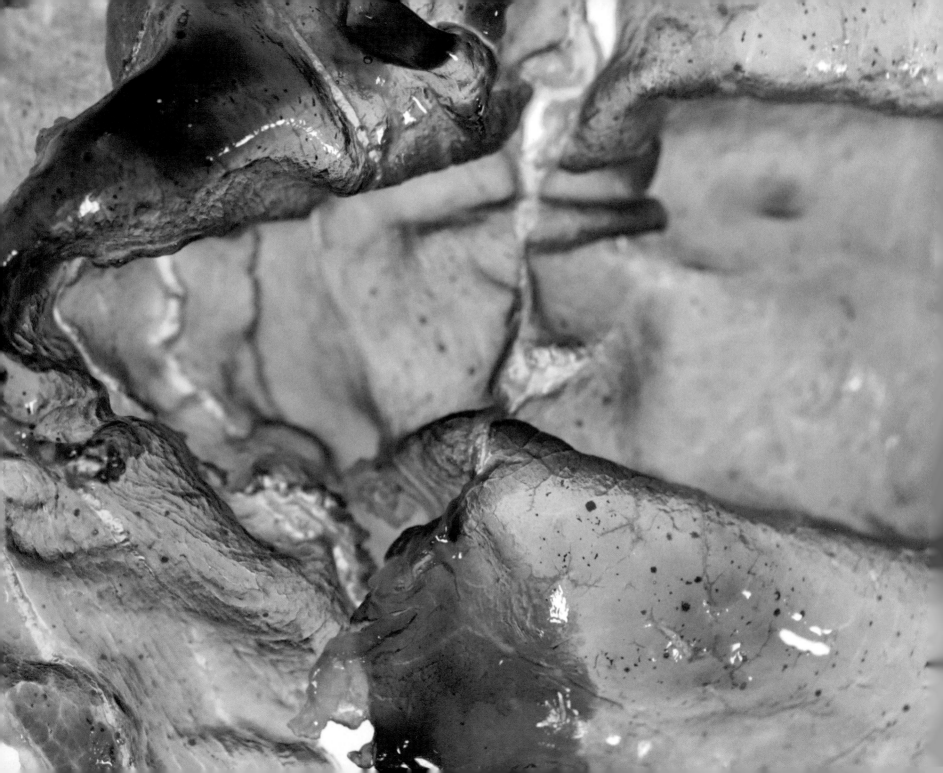

CANDIED PROSCIUTTO

These sweet meat treats are highly addictive. I often serve them with foie gras (see The Inglorious Basquered, page 32) as an added bit of crunch, but they also play nice as an accompaniment to a cheese plate or a salad. ▪ **MAKES 5 SLICES**

1 Preheat the oven to 400°F. Line a baking sheet with foil.

2 Combine the sugar and water in a saucepan. Bring to a simmer over medium heat and cook until fully dissolved. Add the prosciutto to the simple syrup and simmer for a few minutes. Remove it and save the prosciutto simple syrup for making cocktails.

3 Transfer the prosciutto to the baking sheet and bake until browned and crispy, 10 to 15 minutes.

1 cup sugar

½ cup water

5 slices prosciutto or Spanish jamón*

* When I need 4 slices for a burger stack, I always make one extra for snacking.

PORNBURGER QUICKIE:

UNCANNED HEAT

I find Spam, served seared and crispy, is akin to its smoked belly brethren, bacon. To elevate everyday Spam, simply heat a little oil in a pan, and brown both sides. The Maillard reaction (or browning reaction) will do the rest of the heavy lifting. Drain on paper towels and serve hot.

PRO TIP: For "Spam fries": In a deep fryer or a deep heavy-bottomed pan with at least 2 inches of oil, preheat your fry oil to 375°F. Slice your can-shaped mound of Spam lengthwise into ½-inch strips the shape of French fries. Fry until they're crispy. Drain and serve hot. These guys come already salted and go down especially well with an ice-cold beer.

COOKING WITH BAE

For evenly cooked, perfectly crispy bacon every time, ditch the skillet and opt for the oven instead. Simply preheat the oven to 375°F, line a baking sheet with foil for easy cleanup, lay the bacon slices about 1 inch apart, and cook for 15 minutes or to desired level of doneness. This method also allows you to spike your bacon with all sorts of flavors by simply sprinkling with a rub or brushing with a sauce or miso. Don't forget to save your bacon fat for cooking. I have a whole jar in my fridge that I replenish regularly.

JERK BACON RUB

MAKES JUST UNDER ½ CUP
(enough to season one piece of bacon or a whole tray)

- ¼ cup packed light brown sugar
- 1 tablespoon whole allspice, ground
- 2 teaspoons chopped fresh thyme
- 1 teaspoon chili flakes
- 1 teaspoon black pepper
- ½ teaspoon dried minced onion
- ¼ teaspoon ground cinnamon
- ¼ teaspoon ground cloves
- ¼ teaspoon ground cumin
- ¼ teaspoon freshly grated nutmeg
- ¼ teaspoon garlic powder

WHITE MISO PARMESAN BACON RUB

MAKES ENOUGH TO SEASON 1 POUND OF BACON

- 3 tablespoons white miso paste
- 2 tablespoons freshly grated Parmesan cheese
- 1 teaspoon black pepper

JALAPEÑO BACON RUB

MAKES ENOUGH TO SEASON 1 POUND OF BACON

- 1 tablespoon jalapeño powder
- 1 teaspoon black pepper
- ¼ teaspoon garlic powder

PUMPK'N SPICE BACON RUB

MAKES ENOUGH TO SEASON 1 POUND OF BACON

Bacon can be from all sorts of parts, places, and animals. I find this rub goes exceptionally well with cured duck bacon, available on www.dartagnan.com.

- ½ teaspoon ground nutmeg
- ½ teaspoon ground cloves
- ½ teaspoon cinnamon
- 1 teaspoon ginger powder
- 3 teaspoons dark brown sugar

COFFEE BACON (AND BURGER) RUB

MAKES ENOUGH TO SEASON 1 POUND OF BACON

- 2 teaspoons finely ground coffee
- 1 teaspoon smoked sweet paprika
- 1 teaspoon dark brown sugar
- 1 teaspoon kosher salt
- ½ teaspoon black pepper
- ½ teaspoon chili flakes
- ½ teaspoon urfa biber pepper*

* Available at a spice store or online.

PORNBURGER QUICKIE:

THE LEGEND OF SPAM

The Hoff might be a commodity in Deutschland, but Spam has got the Pacific Islands on lockdown. The slogan for destinations like Guam, Hawaii, and the Philippines might as well be "When you're here, you're Spamily." The potted meat has rooted itself in everything from traditional dishes like Spam musubi (marinated and seared Spam on rice, wrapped in nori) to breakfast beasts like Burger King's Spam Croissan'wich.

How many other "miracle meats" out there can actually say they helped win a World War? Spam is a motherfucking legend in a potted league of its own—a national goddamn treasure.

CARNITAS

Carnitas, literally "little meats," offer the opulence of a French confit by way of Mexican flavors and culinary traditions. Good carnitas are simultaneously juicy, tender, and crispy. They're also the metric I use when evaluating a new taqueria. This recipe works as well inside a taco as it does on top of a burger. ▪ **MAKES ROUGHLY 1 QUART**

1 Make the carnitas rub: Combine the brown sugar, amarillo pepper, orange zest, urfa biber pepper, black pepper, salt, juniper berries, onion powder, MSG, garlic powder, cayenne, and cinnamon in a spice grinder or mortar and blend into a powder.

2 Make the carnitas: Season the cut pork shoulder cubes liberally with the rub. Let the rub sit on the pork for at least 8 hours, or overnight.

3 Preheat the oven to 275°F.

4 Stuff the seasoned pork shoulder, bay leaf, garlic, and shallot in a large cast-iron or heavy-bottomed pan so that almost no space remains. Pour in the lard so that it completely covers the pork and effectively fills in the spaces between ingredients. Cover the pan with foil and place in the oven. Cook until the pork is tender and falling apart, 3½ to 4 hours.

5 Use a slotted spoon to remove the pork from the pan. Place the carnitas in a sealable container. Strain the cooking fat through a sieve and pour over the pork to cover. This will help preserve the shelf life of the carnitas as well as juiciness.

6 When you're ready to serve, shred the chunks using your fingers. Preheat a pan over medium heat, with a little of the reserved carnitas fat. Add the shredded pork and cook until slightly crispy but still juicy and tender. Season with salt and pepper to taste. Serve hot.

CARNITAS RUB:
- 2 tablespoons light brown sugar
- 2 tablespoons powdered ají amarillo pepper*
- 1 tablespoon grated orange zest
- 1 tablespoon urfa biber pepper*
- 1 tablespoon black pepper
- 1 tablespoon kosher salt
- 1 teaspoon juniper berries*
- 1 teaspoon onion powder
- 1 teaspoon MSG
- ½ teaspoon garlic powder
- ½ teaspoon cayenne pepper
- ½ teaspoon ground cinnamon

CARNITAS:
- 3 pounds boneless pork shoulder, roughly cut into 2- to 3-inch cubes
- 1 bay leaf
- 5 cloves garlic
- 1 shallot
- 2 cups lard, melted, or vegetable oil
- Kosher salt and black pepper

Available at a spice store or online

BEER-BRAISED PORK CHEEKS

Let's be honest. I could close my eyes, point at a butchered pig, and be satisfied with whichever cut resulted. That said, pork cheeks are about as good as it gets. Born to be braised, pork cheeks stand out as uniquely tender, while being incredulously lean and full of flavor. ▪ **MAKES ROUGHLY 1 QUART**

1 Preheat the oven to 300°F.

2 Combine the flour, salt, and black pepper in a small bowl. Remove any remaining silver skin from each of the cheeks, and lightly dredge the cheeks in the flour mixture.

3 Preheat a large cast-iron or heavy-bottomed pot over high heat with 1 tablespoon of the olive oil. Sear each side of the cheeks in the pot. Once browned, set aside and allow the meat to rest. You can do this in batches, if need be.

4 In the same pot, heat the remaining tablespoon of olive oil over medium heat. Add the onion and celery and sauté. Season with a pinch of salt and pepper. Once the onion begins to soften, add the garlic and chiles, stirring as needed. Continue to cook until the garlic is fragrant. Add the pork stock, beer, juniper berries, peppercorns, orange quarters, bay leaf, cilantro, and thyme. You can add more beer (or water) to makes sure the pork cheeks are fully submerged. Bring everything to a boil and cover the pot with foil. Put the pot in the oven and braise until the cheeks are incredibly tender and falling apart, 3 to 4 hours.

5 When they're finished braising, remove the cheeks from the liquid, allowing them to cool slightly. Once you can safely handle the cheeks with your hands, shred them using your fingers, and place in a bowl with a little bit of the braising broth. This will keep the meat nice and succulent.

½ cup all-purpose flour

1 teaspoon kosher salt, plus more for seasoning

1 teaspoon black pepper, plus more for seasoning

2 pounds pork cheek

2 tablespoons extra-virgin olive oil

½ red onion, quartered

2 stalks celery, roughly chopped

2 or 3 cloves garlic, smashed

4 guajillo chiles*

2 cups pork stock

1 can IPA beer

1 teaspoon juniper berries*

1 teaspoon black peppercorns

½ orange, quartered

1 bay leaf

8 sprigs cilantro

6 sprigs thyme

Available at your local grocery store or online.

ON THE
LAMB

LAMB BURGERS

These burgers make living on the lamb exceptionally easy. The recipe below can be cooked stovetop, as indicated, but is also tasty as fuck when f-lamb-broiled on an open grill. ▪ **MAKES 4 BURGERS**

1 Mix the lamb, shallot, garlic, parsley, chili flakes, and allspice together in a bowl so that everything is fully integrated. Run the mix through your grinder, making sure to keep the grind loose. Measure out the patties on a scale, mindful of how you handle the grind, so that they're about 6 ounces each. Form the patties as lightly and with as little pressure as possible to ensure the ideal consistency.

2 Preheat a cast-iron pan over medium-high heat, with a drizzle of olive oil. Season the patties with salt and pepper, and cook the patties like you would beef burgers, flipping on the reg, until you reach your desired level of doneness. I prefer a good medium cook (between 130°–135°F) for lamb. Remember to allow your burgers time to rest before serving.

1½ **pounds ground lamb shoulder,
chilled**
1 **shallot, finely minced**
1 **clove garlic, finely minced**
1 **tablespoon minced fresh parsley**
1 **teaspoon chili flakes**
A pinch of ground allspice
Extra-virgin olive oil, for the pan
Kosher salt and black pepper

SLOW-ROASTED LAMB BELLY

I prepare lamb belly almost exactly the same way I prepare pork belly. Low and slow. ▪ **MAKES 8 TO 16 SERVINGS**

1 Combine the brown sugar, coriander, salt, and pepper in a small bowl. Rub the mixture all over the lamb belly, place in a sealable container, and refrigerate overnight.

2 Preheat the oven to 450°F.

3 Remove the lamb belly from the fridge and discard any liquid. Place the belly, fat side up, on a rimmed baking sheet and cook for 1 hour. Remove the belly from the oven and brush with any accumulated juices.

4 Drop the oven temperature down to 250°F, return the belly to the oven, and continue to cook for 2 more hours, brushing with juices periodically. When the belly is fork-tender, brush each side with the strawberry harissa and continue to cook for 15 minutes. Remove the belly from the oven and allow to cool. For clean-cut pieces, wrap the cooled belly in plastic wrap and refrigerate before slicing.

5 To serve, simply slice and sear each side in a skillet over medium-high heat, about 2 minutes per side. Brush again with strawberry harissa before serving.

¼ cup packed light brown sugar
1 teaspoon coriander seed, toasted
2 tablespoons kosher salt
1 teaspoon black pepper
2 pounds lamb belly, skin removed
¼ cup Strawberry Harissa (page 180)

HARVEY'S MARKET, DC

UNION MARKET, 1309 5TH STREET NE, WASHINGTON, DC 20002

Brothers in butchery, George Lesznar and Marty Kaufman believe in two things: happy animals and happy customers. It's a refreshingly simple approach that translates to a win-win for everybody involved. These meat magicians have focused their model around sourcing locally raised meat, from family-owned, sustainable farms. Better yet, they personally visit each farm to talk to the farmers and see how their animals are being raised. And for the customer side of things? It turns out responsibly raised, naturally fed animals make for naturally happy customers (AND burgers).

DEER
PRUDENCE

VENISON BURGERS

For some people, venison's rogue, wild flavors can be a turnoff. To that I say, "Don't hate the player, hate the game." Gaminess has a direct correlation to the deer's diet—a farm-raised deer, given a steady diet of corn, is going to be inherently milder in flavor than your average wild buck that's foraged the forest floors, so shop accordingly. That said, I personally love a little "game" and have seasoned these burgers to "lean into," rather than mask, venison's more woodsy notes. ▪ **MAKES 4 BISTRO-SIZE BURGERS**

1 Mix the venison, shallot, garlic, parsley, Worcestershire sauce, sesame oil, and allspice together in a bowl so that everything is fully integrated. Run the mix through your grinder, making sure to keep the grind loose. Carefully measure out the patties on a scale so that they're about 6 ounces each. Form the patties with a light touch and season liberally with salt and pepper.

2 Preheat a cast-iron pan over high heat and drizzle with the oil. Once the pan is smoking, add the patties and drop the heat to medium. Flip the patties every 30 seconds or so, until you reach your desired level of doneness. I prefer a good medium-rare cook on venison, about 3 to 4 minutes.

1½ pounds ground venison (preferably shoulder), chilled*

1 shallot (2 cloves), finely minced

1 clove garlic, finely minced

1 tablespoon minced fresh parsley

1 teaspoon Worcestershire sauce

½ teaspoon sesame oil

A pinch of ground allspice

Kosher salt and black pepper

1 or 2 tablespoons extra-virgin olive oil, for the pan

If only tenderloin is available, combine 1¼ pounds ground tenderloin with 4 ounces ground bacon (about 3 slices).

FOWL
PLAY

SEARED FOIE GRAS

This is foie-r and away my favorite way to prepare this delicacy. It's also the easiest. I prefer to use grade-A foie gras lobes that I purchase from Hudson Valley Foie Gras. On average, a lobe weighs about 1½ pounds and can serve close to ten people. Depending on what you're using it for, I often buy the "cubed" foie gras, which comes precut in odd shapes, but is often suitable for throwing on a burger. The cubes are not as pretty, but they're certainly a lot cheaper. Uncooked foie freezes nicely and can be saved for later use.

If you've purchased a whole lobe, start by cutting it into 1-inch-thick slices. Score both sides of each slice by cutting shallow diagonal lines, to make a crosshatch design. When you're ready to sear, get a heavy pan ripping hot over high heat. No fat is needed because, as you'll see, foie is basically all fat. Liberally season each side with salt and black pepper and lay it in the pan. There will be smoke. Foie-get-about it. The cooking is fast. We're looking for deeply browned, crispy edges, which should only take 30 to 45 seconds. Using a spatula, flip the foie and sear for another 30 to 45 seconds, or until nicely browned. Remove from the heat, and allow to rest on a plate lined with paper towels for a couple of minutes before serving.

PORNBURGER QUICKIE:

FOIE GRAS

Foie. Gras. Two little words that have a tendency to evoke a whole lot of passion, and rightfully so. On one hand, it's foie-cking delicious. On the other, we've all seen and/or heard the horror stories of how geese and ducks are raised on commercial farms in Canada and France. I like my pleasures guilty as much as the next person; however, I never acquired a taste for senseless animal torture. Thankfully, that's a pill that Americans no longer have to swallow. Artisanal farms like Hudson Valley Foie Gras and La Belle Farms are elevating the ethical foie game with responsibly raised fowl. We're talking spaciously housed, cage-free moulard ducks hand-fed by workers incentivized to treat the ducks with a gentle touch. If you ever find yourself in the Hudson Valley area, I recommend a tour. Both farms are refreshingly transparent in their operations, and their foie is dangerously delicious. For most of us who are not in the area, they ship nationwide. High five, Internet!

WWW.HUDSONVALLEYFOIEGRAS.COM
WWW.LABELLEFARMS.COM

DUCK BURGERS AU POIVRE

Duck . . . it's the "other" red meat. While ducks are extremely fatty, their muscles are not. This is exactly why you grind in a little extra rendered fat to ensure juiciness. (I've also never said "no" to anything duck fat.) These burgers work well on their own or "au poivre." I should note, however, that if you do make them au poivre, a little cream sauce of sorts (see Foie Gras Cognac Sauce, page 185) will help balance the powerful notes of pepper.

▪ MAKES 4 BURGERS

1 Toss the ground duck with the ¼ cup rendered duck fat, the shallot, garlic, and sesame oil. Run the mix through the grinder, using the large die (bigger holes). Gently form your patties, dividing the ground duck evenly into four 6-ounce patties.

2 Combine the peppercorns and coarsely grind them using a mortar and pestle (or by hand with a chef's knife if need be).

3 Preheat a cast-iron skillet over medium heat, with the 2 tablespoons duck fat. Season the duck patties with Worcestershire powder (if using) and a pinch of salt, then carefully impress both sides of the patties into the peppercorns. Sear the patties, flipping regularly, until you reach a desired level of doneness. I prefer to cook my duck to medium-rare.*

*The USDA recommends cooking duck breasts to an internal temperature of 165°F to ensure that any harmful bacteria are killed, but I prefer to cook them to only 135°F.

1½ pounds duck breast, skinned and ground

¼ cup rendered duck fat,** plus 2 tablespoons for cooking

1 shallot, finely minced

1 clove garlic, finely minced

1 teaspoon sesame oil

1 tablespoon black peppercorns

3 tablespoons pink peppercorns

3 tablespoons green peppercorns

Worcestershire powder (optional)

Kosher salt

** Available at some grocers and butchers, and online

EGGERS CAN BE CHOOSERS

You better believe I egg on the reg. Here are some of my favorite ways to prepare.

SOUS-VIDE POACHED EGGS:

I've tried just about every method out there, and I find the technique adapted from both ChefSteps and Chef J. Kenji Lopez to be essentially foolproof, allowing you to "poach" several eggs at once. Simply set your sous-vide water bath to 167°F using the immersion circulator. When your water is at temp, place your egg(s)—still in their shells—in the bath and cook for 14 minutes. When they're done, gently crack and drain them onto a slotted spoon. Don't have an immersion circulator? Heat water to about 173°F and pour it into a small insulated cooler or thermos. Add the egg(s) and let cook for the same period of time.

FRIED EGGS:

I like my fried eggs a little crispy, with browned edges and a runny yolk. To achieve this, I start with my broiler set to high and add 2 to 3 tablespoons of olive oil to a small skillet over medium-high heat. Once the oil begins to shimmer, I gently crack my egg into the pan and allow it to cook without touching it. As the whites set and the edges begin to crisp (you should be able to swirl it around the pan without sticking), I take the pan and throw it under the direct heat of the broiler, until the whites covering the yolk start to set, about 1 minute tops.

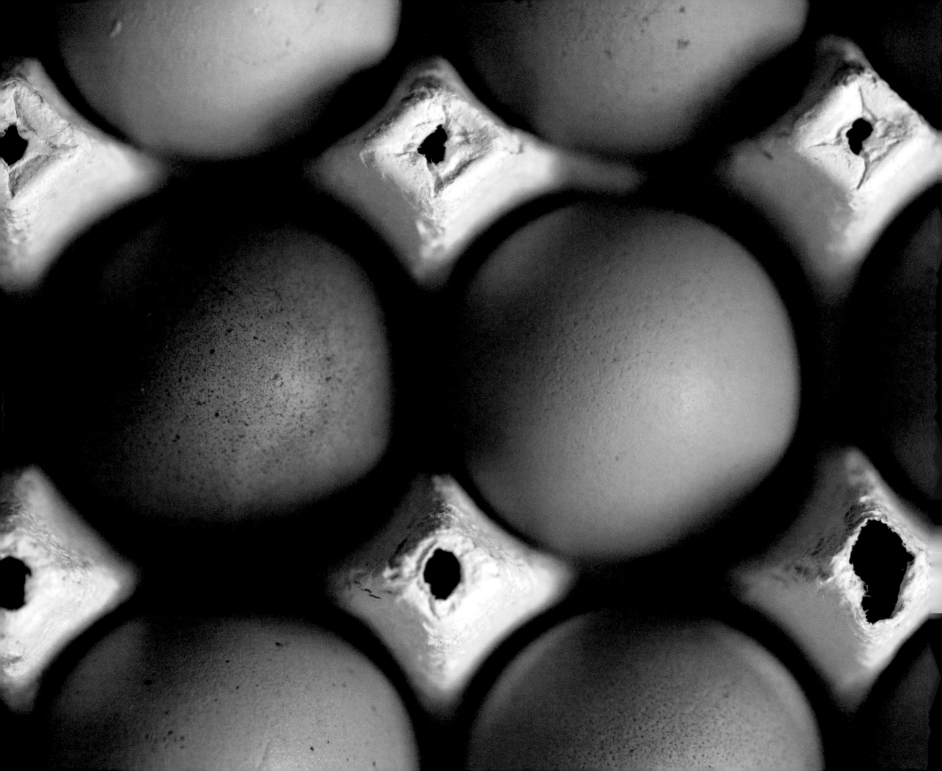

PORNBURGER QUICKIE:

BORN THIS WAY

Fine, I'll say it. Duck eggs are annoying. Good at everything, their only fault is that they have no faults. You know the type. Put a photograph of a chicken egg next to one of a duck egg, and they'll look like "before" and "after" shots, highlighting the transformation from average to eggceptional.

Don't get me wrong—chickens have got a good thing going, but the heftier girth of duck eggs indicates that bigger is indeed better. Not only do they have twice the nutrients, but they're also filthy rich in creamy flavor and yolk-popp'n action, AND they make for great baked-good fluffers. On top of that, their thicker shell makes them impervious to insult, AND gives them a longer shelf life. In recipes, I substitute one duck egg for one chicken egg. For recipes that require a lot of eggs, I substitute three duck eggs for every four chicken eggs.

FRIED CHICKEN

In the South, where fried food is religion, chicken is God. Forget KFC's top-secret blend of eleven herbs and spices; fried chicken success is ALL about dat brine. For this recipe, we bathe the beauties in pickle juice to impart flavor and ensure a good level of juiciness. ▪ **MAKES 6 SERVINGS**

1 Brine the chicken: In a medium pot, combine the water, pickle juice, sugar, and salt. Set over medium heat and stir until the sugar and salt have dissolved. Remove from the heat and allow to cool to room temperature. (To speed things up, you can put the pot in an ice bath.) Once the brine has completely cooled, add those beautiful chicken thighs and refrigerate for at least 6 hours and up to 24 hours.

2 Make the fried chicken: Preheat the oven to 200°F. In a deep fryer or a deep heavy-bottomed pan with at least 2 inches of oil, preheat your fry oil to 300°F (I broke down and bought a personal deep fryer for ease and precision, but a cast-iron pan will do just fine).

3 Now for your dredging station. In one bowl, combine the flour and 2 tablespoons of the fried chicken seasoning. In another bowl, combine the buttermilk with the salt. Remove the thighs from the brine and pat dry. Liberally season them on both sides with the seasoning. For the first pass, dredge all of the chicken thighs in flour. Drizzle a spoon or two of the buttermilk over the flour in the bowl for awesome texture (the bit of buttermilk in the flour creates lumps that create nice "crags" of crunchiness when you fry). Next, take each thigh and fully submerge in the buttermilk, letting the excess drip off before dredging back in the flour. Once fully battered, allow to sit for 5 minutes.

4 Once your oil is at temperature, drop those sexy thighs into the oil and fry until golden brown and crispy, 13 to 15 minutes. If you're using a cast-iron pan, you'll probably have to flip the chicken about 7 minutes in. Remove the fried chicken and drain on a wire rack. You'll probably have to fry in batches, so keep the cooked chicken warm in the oven as you fry the rest.

BRINE AND CHICKEN:
- 3 cups cold water
- 1 cup dill pickle juice*
- 3 tablespoons sugar
- 3 tablespoons kosher salt
- 6 boneless, skinless chicken thighs

FRIED CHICKEN:
- Peanut oil, for deep-frying
- 2 cups all-purpose flour
- ¼ cup Fried Chicken Seasoning (recipe follows)
- 3 cups buttermilk
- 2 pinches of kosher salt

You can use leftover pickle juice from my Quick Pickled Hamburger Dills (page 216), or use store-bought . . . I won't tell.

FRIED CHICKEN SEASONING

MAKES 2/3 CUP

2 tablespoons plus 2 teaspoons sweet paprika

4 teaspoons MSG

4 teaspoons garlic powder

4 teaspoons onion powder

4 teaspoons mustard powder

4 teaspoons kosher salt

2 teaspoons black pepper

2 teaspoons cayenne pepper

Stir everything together in a bowl. Store airtight.

WET 'N' WILD

LOBSTER BURGERS

I'll be the first to admit that lobster is one of those foods that is absolutely perfect by itself. But why settle? Amirite? These burgers are decadent on decadent, so TREAT YO'SELF. ▪ **MAKES 4 BURGERS**

1 Combine the lobster, shrimp, onion, jalapeño, parsley, lemon zest, mayo, and panko in a bowl and gently mix together. Form the mix into four 6-ounce patties, using a buttered ring mold. Place the formed patties on a baking sheet and refrigerate for at least 30 minutes.

2 When you're ready to cook the patties, melt the butter in a cast-iron skillet over medium heat. Lightly dust the patties with flour and carefully place them in the butter. Cook for about 3 minutes on each side, or until they're seared and have some nice color. They are a little delicate, so just be mindful when moving them about. Season with salt and pepper and serve them fresh off the press.

12 ounces steamed or boiled lobster meat (about 4 tails or two 1½-pound lobsters), chopped

½ pound raw shrimp, peeled, deveined, and pureed

½ white onion, finely diced

1 jalapeño, minced

1 tablespoon chopped fresh parsley
Grated zest of 1 lemon

2 tablespoons homemade mayonnaise (page 166)

⅓ cup panko bread crumbs

3 tablespoons butter, or as needed

½ cup all-purpose flour
Kosher salt and black pepper

SMOKED TROUT BURGERS

These smoked trout burgers up the fish fillet sandwich by roughly a gazillion percent. You can adorn them with all the fixin's (see A Fish Called Hitachi Wanda, page 76), but a smear of fresh mayo and a soft brioche bun will also do the trick. ▪ **MAKES 6 BURGERS**

1 Make the onion confit: Preheat the oven to 375°F. In a small baking dish, combine the onions and olive oil. What's important is that the onions are fully submerged in the olive oil. Roast for 40 minutes. Drain the onions and reserve the extremely flavorful olive oil for other uses.

2 Make the smoked trout patties: In a deep fryer or a deep heavy-bottomed pan with at least 2 inches of oil, preheat your fry oil to 325°F.

3 In the meantime, combine the roasted onions, green onions, garlic, tarragon, basil, parsley, lemon zest, lemon juice, capers, mayo, mustard, sambal, salt, pepper, and ½ cup of the bread crumbs in a food processor. Pulse the ingredients until combined.

4 Transfer the puree to a large bowl and fold in the trout and corn, using a rubber spatula. For the sake of texture, be careful not to overwork the mixture.

5 Use a scale to measure out six 4-ounce patties. Shape the patties and roll them in the remaining bread crumbs. Fry until golden brown, about 5 minutes.

ONION CONFIT:
   2 medium yellow onions, sliced
   1 cup extra-virgin olive oil

SMOKED TROUT PATTIES:
   Canola oil, for deep-frying
   ¼ cup green onions, finely chopped
   2 cloves garlic, peeled
   ¼ cup fresh tarragon
   ¼ cup fresh basil
   ¼ cup fresh parsley
   1 lemon, zested and juiced
   1 tablespoon capers
   ⅓ cup homemade mayonnaise (page 166)
   1 tablespoon coarse mustard
   1 teaspoon sambal chili paste
   1 teaspoon kosher salt
   ½ teaspoon black pepper
   1½ cups dried bread crumbs
   1½ pounds Smoked Trout (recipe follows)
   Kernels from 1 ear of corn

RECIPE CONTINUES ▶

SMOKED TROUT

1 Heat up the wood chips in a stovetop smoker over medium-high heat until they begin smoking. Add the trout and seal the smoker. Cook the trout over medium-low heat for 15 minutes. Remove the trout from the heat and allow to cool. Once cool, discard the skins.

2 If you don't have a stovetop smoker, you can make one with a little ingenuity. All you need is a large pot, a steamer insert, and some foil. Put a layer of foil on the bottom of the pot. Add the wood chips, and then cover them with another layer of foil. Place the steamer insert on top, followed by your trout fillets. Heat the wood chips over medium-high heat until they begin smoking, then quickly seal the top of the pot with a tight wrapping of foil to keep the smoke in. Reduce the heat to medium-low and cook for 15 minutes.

1 tablespoon alder wood smoking chips*

1½ pounds trout fillets (about 2)

* Stovetop smokers use a superfine-size wood chip for quick smoking. These are readily available online.

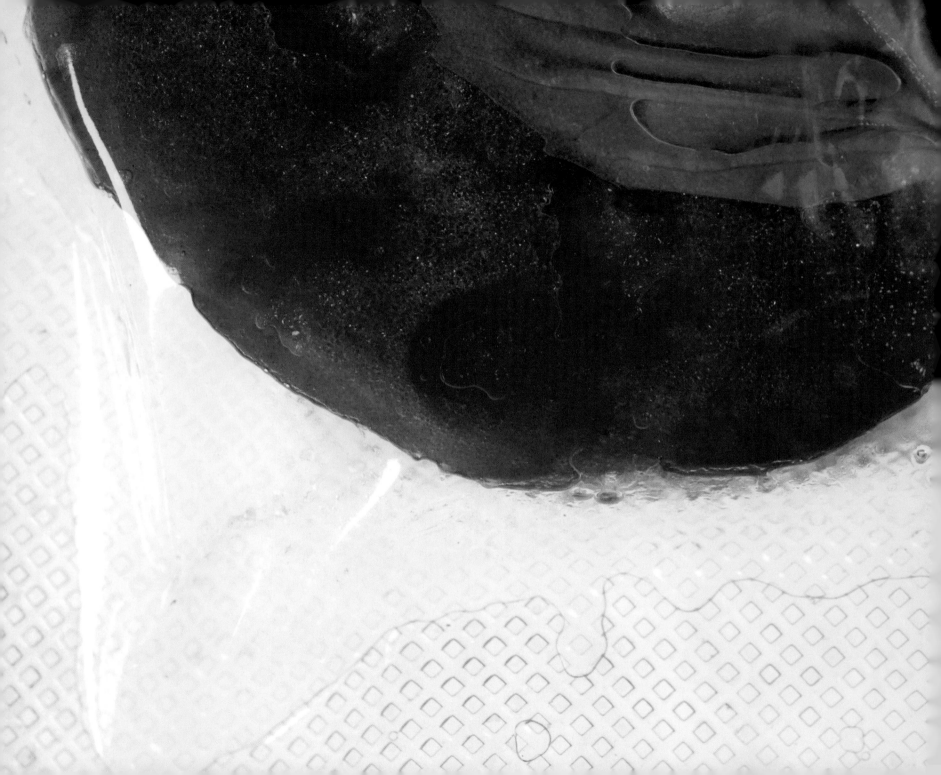

FARM TO
VEG-
TABLE

COMPRESSED WATERMELON PATTIES

These unconventional patties are a refreshing, garden-friendly change of pace. By using a vacuum sealer (as used for cooking sous-vide—see page 12) to marinate the watermelon, we compress its structural integrity, giving the melon a denser, almost "meatier," texture. Goat Cheese Beignets (page 242) are a natural with these melonious patties, but they can also stand on their own as a fun salad course. ▪ **MAKES 4 PATTIES**

Using a 3-inch biscuit cutter, cut the watermelon into rounds. Place the watermelon, lime juice, vinegar, sesame oil, and basil leaves in a vacuum bag and vacuum seal. Place the sealed bag in the refrigerator. To help with the compression, I add a little weight to sit evenly on top (like an 8 x 8-inch cake pan filled with water). Refrigerate the marinating melon for at least 3 hours or overnight. When ready to serve, remove the melon from the bag and season lightly with a pinch of salt.

Four 1-inch-thick slices watermelon
2 tablespoons fresh lime juice
1 tablespoon rice vinegar
½ teaspoon spicy sesame oil
4 basil leaves
Kosher salt

VEGGIE BURGERS

This is probably a safe place to mention that I was a vegetarian for six years. In that period, I ate A LOT of veggie burgers. Most of them pretty "meh." For this recipe I was inspired to create a veggie burger that embraced the earthiness of herbs and beets but had some of the crunch and texture of falafel and absolutely none of the qualities of those dreadful prepackaged soy burgers found at every backyard BBQ ever. Beet, don't kale my vibe.

■ MAKES 6 BURGERS

1 Combine the chickpeas, wheat berries, beets, egg, green onions, cilantro, parsley, garlic, lemon zest, coriander, salt, black pepper, and cayenne in a food processor and pulse. I recommend pulsing 4 to 6 times to get a good consistency. You want the mix to be chunky rather than a smooth puree.

2 Transfer the mixture to a medium bowl and add the olive oil, cornstarch, and panko. Mix the ingredients with your hands until everything is fully incorporated. Form the mixture into 6 patties and refrigerate for 30 minutes. The mixture will be a little loose but should hold when compacted. The time in the fridge will help the patties set.

3 In a deep fryer or a deep heavy-bottomed pan with at least 2 inches of oil, preheat your fry oil to 350°F.

4 When ready to fry, carefully submerge the patties in the hot oil and cook for about 5 minutes. The outside should be nice and crispy to the touch. Season with salt and serve warm.

* To save time, I shred the beets using the shredder attachment of my food processor.

1 cup cooked chickpeas
1 cup cooked wheat berries,
1 cup shredded beets*
1 egg
3 green onions, roughly chopped (about ¼ cup)
¼ cup minced fresh cilantro
¼ cup minced fresh parsley
2 cloves garlic, minced
Grated zest of 1 lemon
1 teaspoon ground coriander
1 teaspoon kosher salt, plus more for seasoning
½ teaspoon black pepper
½ teaspoon cayenne pepper
1 tablespoon extra-virgin olive oil
1 tablespoon cornstarch
½ cup panko bread crumbs
Canola oil, for deep-frying

DOUBLE-FRIED PICKLE "PATTIES"

Simply put, these patties are kind of a big dill. Somebody whiskey me. ▪ **MAKES 4 PATTIES**

1 To make a pickle "patty," skewer 3 spear halves with two toothpicks (one from the left and one from the right). To make the "patty" nice and compact, the two outside pickles should be facing up and the middle one facing down. Repeat until you're out of spears.

2 Drain the "patties" on paper towels (the last thing you want is hot oil splattering in your face as you deep-fry these puppies).

3 In a deep fryer or a deep heavy-bottomed pan with at least 2 inches of oil, preheat your fry oil to 375°F. (It's important to keep the oil hot or your pickles will get mushy.)

4 Set up a dredging station: Combine ½ cup of the flour, 1 teaspoon salt, and 1 teaspoon black pepper in a small bowl. In a second bowl, combine the remaining 1 cup flour and the cornmeal, baking powder, cumin, cayenne, egg, and beer. Whisk the batter until all of the ingredients are fully incorporated.

5 Dredge the pickle patties in the flour mixture and then fully submerge in the beer batter. Carefully place the patties in the hot oil and fry until golden brown. Use tongs to gently handle the patties, as they're a little fragile. Drain the pickle patties on paper towels and allow them to cool and crisp for about a minute.

6 Using the tongs again, take the fried pickle patties and once again submerge them in the beer batter and then the hot oil. That's right, we're double-frying these dudes. Once fried to a golden crisp, remove them from the oil and drain on paper towels. Allow your fried pickles to cool before serving. Season with a sprinkle of salt.

6 dill pickle spears, halved and
    drained on paper towels
1½ cups all-purpose flour
1 teaspoon kosher salt, plus more
    for seasoning
    Black pepper
1 teaspoon black pepper
1 cup cornmeal
1 tablespoon baking powder
1 teaspoon ground cumin
½ teaspoon cayenne pepper
1 large egg, lightly beaten
    One 12-ounce can of IPA-style beer
    Canola oil, for deep-frying

THE PORNBURGER PANTRY

What's in the PornBurger pantry? The best game of seven minutes in heaven you've never played. Also, condiments, sauces, and burger parts to keep you well stocked for a variety of stacks as well as enable your own tangential adventures in eating.

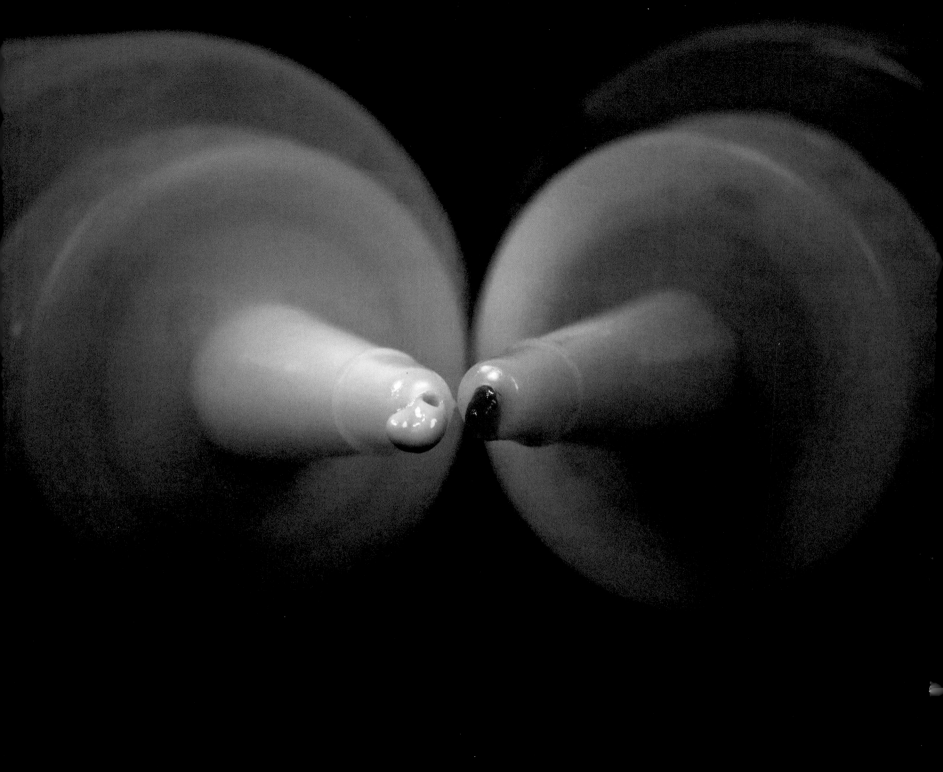

CONDIMENTS

MAYONNAISE-BASED CONDIMENTS

Growing up, I was never much of a mayo fan. That all changed as soon as I started making my own. I like my mayonnaise fresh and bright. This basic recipe is great alone but it's also the building block for a lot of other condiments, as you'll see. I find mayonnaise is easier to make in large batches. That said, this recipe can just be halved or doubled to meet your own needs.

MAYONNAISE

MAKES ABOUT 3 CUPS

4 egg yolks

2 tablespoons plus 2 teaspoons apple cider vinegar

1 teaspoon fresh lemon juice

¼ cup Dijon mustard

½ teaspoon cayenne pepper

1 teaspoon kosher salt

3 cups safflower oil

In culinary school, you learn to make mayonnaise whisking by hand. Fuck that—I recommend using a stand mixer. Combine the yolks, vinegar, lemon juice, mustard, cayenne, and salt in your mixer bowl and mix with the whisk attachment on a medium speed (5 or 6) until combined. Keep the mixer on the same speed and add a few drops of oil at a time, waiting for all the oil to be incorporated before adding more. When the mixture begins to thicken and emulsify, you can start adding a more constant, but thin, stream of oil. Continue until all of the oil has emulsified. Store airtight in the refrigerator for up to 3 weeks.

PORNBURGER SMOKY BURGER SAUCE

MAKES ABOUT 1 CUP

Behind EVERY GREAT BURGER is a super-secret special sauce. This is mine.

¾ cup homemade mayonnaise (at left)

4 teaspoons chili garlic sauce (I like Huy Fong)

2 tablespoons ketchup

1 tablespoon sweet relish*

1 teaspoon liquid smoke

* I use Gordy's Sweet Pepper Relish, which is a blend of pickled cucumbers, celery, onions, and peppers. (For more about Gordy's, see page 13.)

Mix together the mayo, chili garlic sauce, ketchup, relish, and liquid smoke. Store airtight in the refrigerator for up to 2 weeks.

MAYONNAISE

PORNBURGER SMOKY BURGER SAUCE

BLACK GARLIC AIOLI

BLACK GARLIC

HOISIN MAYONNAISE

MAKES ABOUT ½ CUP

If you're in the DC area, I highly recommend Honeycomb's hoisin, house made with locally harvested sweet potatoes.

½ cup homemade mayonnaise (page 166)

2 tablespoons hoisin sauce

Stir the mayo and hoisin together until both ingredients are fully incorporated. Store airtight in the refrigerator for up to 2 weeks.

KIMCHI THOUSAND ISLAND DRESSING

MAKES ABOUT 1 CUP

¾ cup homemade mayonnaise (page 166)

2 tablespoons ketchup

4 teaspoons minced cabbage kimchi

1 tablespoon plus 1 teaspoon red chili paste (I like sambal oelek)

Mix together the mayo, ketchup, kimchi, and chili paste until combined. Store airtight in the refrigerator for up to 2 weeks.

BLACK GARLIC AIOLI

MAKES 1 CUP

1 cup homemade mayonnaise (page 166)

1 bulb black garlic, cloves removed from skins

Place the mayo and black garlic in a food processor and pulse until combined. Store airtight in the refrigerator for up to 2 weeks.

MUSTARD GREEN AIOLI

MAKES ABOUT 1½ CUPS

1 cup homemade mayonnaise (page 166)

1 tablespoon Dijon mustard (page 172)

1 tablespoon Mustard Caviar (page 172)

1 clove garlic, peeled

1 cup roughly chopped mustard greens (ribs removed)

Kosher salt

Combine the mayo, mustard, mustard caviar, garlic, and mustard greens in a food processor and puree until smooth. Taste and season with salt if needed. Store airtight in the refrigerator for up to 2 weeks.

ANCHOVY AIOLI

MAKES ABOUT 1 CUP

1 cup homemade mayonnaise (page 166)

2 olive oil–packed anchovy fillets

1 clove garlic, peeled

1 teaspoon fresh lemon juice

Combine the mayo, anchovies, garlic, and lemon juice in a food processor and puree. Store airtight in the refrigerator for up to 2 weeks.

SUMAC AIOLI

MAKES ABOUT 1¼ CUPS

1 cup homemade mayonnaise (page 166)

1 tablespoon Dijon mustard

1 clove garlic, peeled

3 tablespoons ground sumac

4½ teaspoons fresh lemon juice

½ teaspoon sesame oil

Combine the mayo, mustard, garlic, sumac, lemon juice, and sesame oil in a food processor and process until combined. Store airtight in the refrigerator for up to 2 weeks.

BLACK GARLIC

If you haven't heard, black garlic is kind of having a moment right now. At the heart of this preserved garlic's darkness lie all the trappings of a late-night skin-a-max seduction: deep caramel notes tempered with just enough umami to make Daddy jealous. And the tonguegasms . . . Oooooh, the tonguegasms . . . (Cue sultry sex-aphone music.)

Sexual feelings aside, this Korean dark knight is also filthy, Bruce Wayne rich in antioxidants and cancer-fighting S-Allyl cysteine. Talk about the full package . . . Black garlic is essentially what every young garlic aspires to be when it grows up. Its transformation from white bulb to black butterfly is the result of a low and slow roasting process that takes up to six weeks. When it comes to black garlic, age is beauty.

TARRAGON GREEN GODDESS DRESSING

MAKES 1 PINT

  1 cup homemade mayonnaise (page 166)
  1 avocado, pitted and peeled
  ½ cup fresh tarragon leaves
  ¼ cup fresh flat-leaf parsley leaves
  ¼ cup fresh basil leaves
  ¼ cup buttermilk
  1 teaspoon anchovy paste
  2 green onions
  1 clove garlic, peeled
  1 teaspoon kosher salt
  ½ teaspoon black pepper

Combine the mayo, avocado, tarragon, parsley, basil, buttermilk, anchovy paste, green onions, garlic, salt, and pepper in a food processor and pulse until combined. Store airtight in the refrigerator for up to 1 week, although avocados will start to change their color after a few days.

PUMPKIN AIOLI

MAKES 1 PINT

  1 cup homemade mayonnaise (page 166)
  1 clove garlic, peeled
  1 cup canned, unsweetened pumpkin puree
  ½ teaspoon smoked sweet paprika
  2 pinches of kosher salt
  ½ teaspoon fresh lemon juice

Combine the mayo, garlic, pumpkin puree, paprika, salt, and lemon juice in a food processor and blend until smooth. Store airtight in the refrigerator for up to 2 weeks.

ANCHOVIES

DIJON MUSTARD

MUSTARD GREEN AIOLI

MUSTARD CAVIAR

MUSTARD-BASED CONDIMENTS

DIJON MUSTARD

MAKES ABOUT 1 PINT

Making homemade mustard couldn't be easier. However, the fresh stuff is incredibly bitter out of the gate, so give it at least 12 hours for the flavors to mellow out. That said, you've got time. Mustard is extremely antibacterial, so your homemade batch should last for at least a year. As it ages, it will also thicken. Simply add a little water to get it back to the desired consistency.

6 tablespoons yellow mustard seeds
½ cup mustard powder
½ teaspoon onion powder
¼ teaspoon garlic powder
2 teaspoons kosher salt
½ cup dry white wine*
3 tablespoons apple cider vinegar
2 tablespoons honey

White wine is traditionally used for Dijon-style mustard, but you can also use a nice hoppy beer, or just some plain-Jane water.

Pulse the mustard seeds a few times in a spice grinder. The idea is not to pulverize them, but rather to just crack some open. Transfer the seeds to a small bowl and add the mustard powder, onion powder, garlic powder, salt, white wine, vinegar, and honey. Stir to incorporate. Store airtight in the refrigerator for at least 12 hours before using.

SRIRACHA MUSTARD: Add 2 teaspoons Sriracha powder.

MUSTARD CAVIAR

MAKES ABOUT 1 CUP

¼ cup yellow mustard seeds
¼ cup brown mustard seeds
1 teaspoon ground turmeric
⅛ teaspoon caraway seeds
¼ cup sugar
½ teaspoon kosher salt
½ cup apple cider vinegar

Stir together the mustard seeds, turmeric, caraway seeds, sugar, salt, and vinegar in a sealable container. Refrigerate for at least 48 hours before using.

BACON MUSTARD

MAKES ABOUT ¾ CUP

½ cup Dijon mustard
1 tablespoon cream-style horseradish
1 tablespoon honey
6 slices thick-cut hickory-smoked bacon, cooked super crispy and crumbled

Mix together the mustard, horseradish, honey, and bacon. Make at least a day in advance for more pronounced flavor. Store airtight in the refrigerator for up to 2 weeks.

KETCHUP-BASED CONDIMENTS

TOMATO KETCHUP

MAKES ABOUT 3 CUPS

More often than not I actually hate homemade ketchups. I mean, just give me that fancy Heinz stuff already! Why bother making my own ketchup, you ask? Pride, namely. There is a certain satisfaction that comes from squirting your own homemade ketchup on a brioche bun you baked, with a burger you ground and seared to perfection.

But, ALSO, this recipe is not like those other homemade ketchups. It actually tastes like store-bought ketchup (if not better), without all the bullshit corn syrup and preservatives. I certainly won't fault you for going the store-bought route, but trust me . . . when you're ready, I got you.

12 ounces tomato paste

¾ cup plus 2 tablespoons distilled white vinegar

¼ cup plus 1 tablespoon water

¼ cup honey

¼ cup sugar

1 teaspoon kosher salt

⅛ teaspoon ground cloves

⅛ teaspoon ground cinnamon

1 teaspoon MSG

Combine the tomato paste, vinegar, water, honey, sugar, salt, cloves, cinnamon, and MSG in a blender and puree until smooth. Transfer the ketchup to a squeeze bottle and high-five yourself for a job well done. It's that easy. Store airtight in the refrigerator for up to 2 weeks.

BROWN KETCHUP

MAKES ½ CUP

¼ cup ketchup

¼ cup HP Sauce*

Commonly available in the international food section of your grocery or online

Mix together the ketchup and HP sauce in a small bowl until combined. Store airtight in the refrigerator for up to 2 weeks.

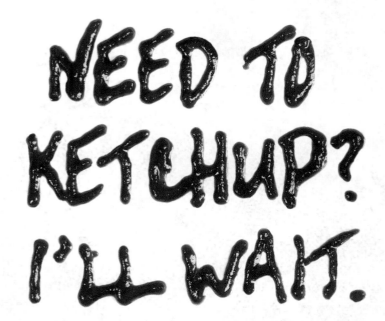
NEED TO KETCHUP? I'LL WAIT.

KIMCHI KETCHUP

MAKES 1 CUP

Top Chef and burger aficionado Richard Blais turned me on to this umami bomb when we joined forces last year in a quest to make the ultimate burger. I like to think of it as a slight hat tip to the condiment's fermented origins.

½ cup napa cabbage kimchi*

½ cup ketchup

½ teaspoon fish sauce

1 teaspoon Sriracha sauce

Napa cabbage kimchi is a good jumping-off point, but certainly not the end-all for this recipe. If you're in the DC area, Honeycomb Grocer (see page 276) makes a spectacular array of seasonally sourced kimchis that would work well. Have fun. Experiment.

Combine the kimchi, ketchup, fish sauce, and Sriracha in a food processor and puree. Store airtight in the refrigerator for up to 2 weeks.

SPRING PEA KETCHUP

MAKES ABOUT 3 CUPS

4 tomatillos, husks on

2 cups fresh peas

4 green onions

¼ cup fresh mint leaves

1 clove garlic, peeled

3 tablespoons fresh lemon juice

1 tablespoon sugar

1 teaspoon kosher salt

1 Preheat the oven to 375°F.

2 Put the tomatillos on a baking sheet and roast until soft and juicy, about 20 minutes. Allow to cool before removing the outer husks.

3 Meanwhile, bring a pot of salted water to a boil and add the peas. Blanch them in the water until soft, 3 to 5 minutes. Drain the peas and transfer them to a food processor.

4 Add the tomatillos, green onions, mint, garlic, lemon juice, sugar, and salt to the food processor and puree. Strain the puree through a fine-mesh sieve. Store the ketchup airtight in the refrigerator for up to 2 weeks.

MUMBO SAUCE

MAKES 1 PINT

You say mambo, I say mumbo. Like its DC brethren the half-smoke, mumbo sauce is a District culinary tradition, whose flavor profile AND spelling differ depending on what late-night joint you frequent. Mumbo sauce can run the spectrum from a gelatinous sweet-and-sour sauce to straight-up BBQ sauce. My version falls heavier on the latter—smoky, sweet, with a bit of tang. At the end of the day, the only rule of mumbo sauce is that it pair nicely with a cool buzz, French fries, and a greasy order of crispy-fried chicken wings.

¾ cup ketchup

½ cup honey

¼ cup Sriracha sauce

½ teaspoon smoked sweet paprika

2 tablespoons apple cider vinegar

1 teaspoon Worcestershire sauce

Whisk together the ketchup, honey, Sriracha, paprika, vinegar, and Worcestershire sauce in a bowl until combined. Store airtight in the refrigerator for up to 2 weeks.

KETCHUP HISTORY

Nothing lights up the sensory spectrum like a good ol'-fashioned tomato ketchup. Salty, sweet, sour, bitter, and umami competitively humping your taste buds for dominance toward a surprisingly balanced result. Chinese in origin, *ke-tchup* actually meant "preserved-fish sauce" in Hokkien, the language of the southern Fujian province and Taiwan. In fact, tomatoes weren't even a part of the fancy sauce equation until 1812, when Philadelphia scientist and horticulturist James Mease published the first tomato ketchup recipe. Today, Heinz sells over eleven billion packets of the red stuff a year. I don't care what the Catholic Church says, condom-ints are totally crucial, which is why I always keep a spare in my wallet. You know . . . just in case.

SAUCES & SPREADS

AVOCADO CREMA

MAKES ABOUT 3 CUPS

 2 avocados, pitted and peeled

½ cup sour cream

¼ cup cilantro leaves

 1 jalapeño, seeds and ribs removed

 1 clove garlic, peeled

 2 limes, juiced

 2 pinches of kosher salt

Combine the avocados, sour cream, cilantro, jalapeño, garlic, lime juice, and salt in a food processor and puree until totally incorporated. Store airtight in the refrigerator for up to 1 week.

GRILLED PINEAPPLE BUTTER

MAKES 2 STICKS OF BUTTER (8 OUNCES)

Burgers, scones, bacon toast . . . as if you needed any extra reasons to eat butter. This semi-sweet, semi-smoky compound plays nice with just about all things salty.

 2 tablespoons canola oil, for grilling

 8 pineapple rings, sliced ½ inch thick

10 tablespoons (5 ounces) salted butter

 1 tablespoon fresh lime juice

½ teaspoon kosher salt

1 Preheat a grill over high heat. Use a brush to lightly oil both the grill grates and the pineapple slices with canola oil.

2 Cook the slices for about 5 minutes on each side, so that they cook through and get some color. The charred bits will add some nice flavor. Remove the slices from the heat and allow to cool to room temperature.

3 Transfer the grilled pineapple to a food processor. Add the butter, lime juice, and salt. Puree until smooth. Store airtight in the refrigerator for up to 1 week.

ROASTED PHYSALIS SHALLOT COMPOTE

MAKES ABOUT 4 SERVINGS (½ CUP)

 1 pint ground cherries (aka cape gooseberries or physalis), husks removed*

 1 medium shallot clove, sliced thin

 2 tablespoons extra-virgin olive oil

 1 teaspoon sugar

 1 tablespoon rice vinegar

 Pinch of kosher salt

* Ground cherries often arrive as a part of the late-summer/early-fall bounty at my local farmers' market. I've also found them at Whole Foods. While physalis are pretty unique in flavor, actual cherries, like the Rainer varietal, would also work.

Preheat your oven to 375°F. Place the ground cherries on a baking sheet and roast for 15 minutes, or until soft. As the cherries roast, sauté the shallot in the olive oil over medium heat until translucent. Transfer the ground cherries, shallot (with olive oil), sugar, and vinegar to a blender and puree. Add the puree to a small pan and reduce the mixture until it begins to thicken, stirring frequently. Season with a pinch of salt. Allow the compote to cool completely before serving. Store airtight in the refrigerator for up to 2 weeks.

GRILLED PINEAPPLES

GRILLED PINEAPPLE BUTTER

PHYSALIS

BACON JAM

STRAWBERRY HARISSA

MAKES 1 PINT

This spread goes exceptionally well with grilled meats, all things feta, AND anything in the mint family (basil, tarragon, etc.).

- 4 dried ancho chiles
- 4 dried guajillo chiles (New Mexico chiles will also work)
- ½ pound strawberries, stems cut off
- 3 sun-dried tomatoes packed in olive oil, drained
- 3 tablespoons extra-virgin olive oil
- 2 teaspoons sugar
- 1½ teaspoons coarse or kosher salt
- 1 teaspoon coriander seeds, toasted and ground
- 1 teaspoon caraway seeds, toasted and ground
- 1 teaspoon cumin seeds, toasted and ground
- 1 teaspoon black vinegar
- 1 lemon, juiced
- Black pepper

In large covered bowl filled with hot water, rehydrate all of the chiles for 15 to 20 minutes. Drain the chiles on paper towels and remove the stems. Add the chiles, strawberries, sun-dried tomatoes, olive oil, sugar, salt, all the seeds, the black vinegar, lemon juice, and pepper to a food processor and puree until smooth. You might have to stop occasionally to scrape the sides with a spatula. Store the harissa in a sealable container in the refrigerator for up to 2 weeks.

CORNICHON RELISH

MAKES ABOUT ¾ CUP

- ¼ cup chopped cornichon pickles
- 3 tablespoons diced peeled cucumber
- ½ small shallot, minced
- 1 clove garlic, minced
- 1 tablespoon chopped fresh parsley
- 1 teaspoon Mustard Caviar (page 172) or whole-grain Dijon mustard
- 1 teaspoon balsamic vinegar
- 1 tablespoon extra-virgin olive oil

Mix together the pickles, cucumber, shallot, garlic, parsley, mustard caviar, balsamic vinegar, and olive oil in a bowl until combined. Store airtight in the refrigerator for up to 2 weeks.

BACON JAM

MAKES ABOUT 3 CUPS

1 pound bacon, cut into 1-inch pieces

4 yellow onions, cut into ¼-inch-thick slices

2 cloves garlic, minced

½ cup black vinegar

1 tablespoon Worcestershire sauce

1 tablespoon HP Sauce*

1 tablespoon pure maple syrup

1 tablespoon Dijon mustard

Kosher salt and black pepper

Commonly available in the international section of your grocery store

1 Toss all of the bacon into a cast-iron skillet and cook over medium heat until most of the fat has rendered and the bacon begins to crisp, about 30 minutes. Stir frequently. If the bacon starts to stick to the bottom of the pan, you can carefully add some water to deglaze as the bacon cooks down. The fat will still render and the water will boil off. With a slotted spoon, transfer the bacon to paper towels to drain. Pour off all but about 3 tablespoons of fat from the skillet. Save the extra bacon fat for cooking with other recipes.

2 Add the onions to the skillet with the remaining bacon fat and sauté over medium heat until translucent, 5 to 7 minutes. Add the garlic and cook until fragrant, about 1 minute. Stir in the bacon, vinegar, Worcestershire sauce, HP Sauce, maple syrup, and mustard. Cook the liquid over medium-low heat until it becomes thick and syrupy, about 30 minutes. Stir occasionally to prevent anything from sticking to the bottom. Season to taste with salt and pepper.

3 Transfer the mixture to a food processor or blender and pulse into a coarse jam. Store airtight in the refrigerator for up to 4 weeks.

PORT WINE ONION JAM

MAKES ABOUT 1 CUP

1 tablespoon salted butter

2 tablespoons extra-virgin olive oil

4 onions, sliced

1 cup port wine

3 tablespoons balsamic vinegar

1 tablespoon Worcestershire sauce

½ teaspoon sugar

Kosher salt

Melt the butter in the oil in a cast-iron skillet or heavy-bottomed pan over low heat. Once the butter has melted, add the onions. Stir the onions as they begin to sweat and lose moisture, continuing to do so regularly, until they are a rich brown color. As the onions' natural sugars begin to caramelize, add the port, vinegar, Worcestershire sauce, and sugar. Continue to cook the onions until the liquid reduces almost completely. The onions will be tender and almost "jammy" in texture. Remove from the heat and season to taste with salt. Keep coarse or for a smoother texture puree in a food processor. Store airtight in the refrigerator for up to 1 month.

BONE MARROW ONION JAM

MAKES ABOUT 1 CUP

4 marrow bones (2 to 2½ pounds)
3 red onions, thinly sliced
1 cup beef stock
¼ cup balsamic vinegar
1 tablespoon Worcestershire sauce
2 cloves garlic, minced
½ teaspoon minced fresh thyme
⅛ teaspoon ground cinnamon
  Kosher salt and black pepper

1 Preheat the oven to 400°F.

2 Arrange the marrow bones on a baking sheet, wide side down, and roast until bubbling, about 20 minutes. Allow to cool for at least 5 minutes before handling.

3 Using a spoon, scoop the marrow from the bones into a small bowl.

4 Preheat a cast-iron skillet over medium heat. Transfer the marrow to the skillet and add the onions. As the marrow cooks, it will render into a super-savory beef-flavored fat. Sauté the onions with the marrow until the onions begin to caramelize.

5 Add the stock, vinegar, Worcestershire sauce, garlic, thyme, and cinnamon to the pan and continue to simmer until the liquid has reduced almost completely, about 30 minutes. Season to taste with salt and pepper. There will be some remaining excess grease with the onions. Drain the jam with a fine-mesh sieve to expel the extra fat and discard it. Allow the jam to cool for 20 minutes before serving. Store airtight in the refrigerator for up to 2 weeks.

BACON PEANUT BUTTER

MAKES ABOUT 1¼ CUPS

1 cup peanut butter (store-bought or homemade using your favorite recipe)
8 slices hickory-smoked bacon, crisp-cooked and crumbled
1 tablespoon bacon fat, reserved from cooking bacon

In a small saucepan, combine the peanut butter, cooked bacon, and bacon fat and warm over medium heat, stirring frequently. Once the mixture begins to bubble, remove from the heat. Allow to cool. Store airtight in the refrigerator for up to 1 month.

BONE MARROW

"I wanted to live deep and suck out all the marrow of life."
—HENRY DAVID THOREAU

What a dude. I think Thoreau's sentiment can best be paraphrased as "Let's bone." And why not? Bone marrow is cheap, easy to prepare, nutrient packed, and, most important, tasty as fuck. For the longest time, Americans have written marrow off as nothing more than dog food, while cultures all over the world have embraced the delicacy with open arms and a softie. (The French even have a special spoon for it!) Kind of makes you wonder what else the canine population has been hiding from us, those smug pugs.

Thankfully, that dark period is behind us and bone is the new black. Depending on how you want to prepare it, ask your butcher to slice it horizontally or vertically into 3-inch pieces. From savory broths to roasted spreads, the marrow of life is truly ripe for the sucking. Plus it comes with a built-in straw, like nature's very own Capri Sun.

BONE MARROW ONION JAM

TRUFFLE WHIPPED GOAT CHEESE

FOIE GRAS COGNAC SAUCE

BOOZY CHEESE SAUCE

FOIE GRAS MOUSSE

MAKES ABOUT 1 PINT

1-pound lobe foie gras (grade A)*

3 tablespoons heavy cream

3 tablespoons Sauternes

Kosher salt and black pepper

See info on foie gras purveyors on page 141. I also order online from D'Artagnan Foods, at www.dartagnan.com.

Place the foie gras, cream, and Sauternes in a food processor and puree until smooth. Season with salt and pepper and push the mousse through a fine-mesh sieve. Serve at room temperature. Store airtight in the refrigerator for up to 1 week.

FOIE GRAS COGNAC SAUCE

MAKES ABOUT 2 CUPS

1 tablespoon butter

1 shallot, minced

1 cup oyster mushrooms

1 cup chicken stock

½ cup cognac

¼ cup port wine

4 ounces foie gras (Grade A), roughly chopped

½ cup heavy (whipping) cream

Kosher salt and black pepper

1 Melt the butter in a medium saucepan over medium heat. Add the shallot and sauté until translucent. Add the mushrooms and sauté until the mushrooms have softened, about 5 minutes. Add the chicken stock, cognac, and port, and simmer until reduced by half. Add the foie gras, stirring until the foie has melted.

2 Pour the sauce through a fine-mesh sieve and return to the saucepan over low heat. Gently pour in the cream and stir until incorporated. Season to taste with salt and pepper and keep warm until ready to serve.

TRUFFLE WHIPPED GOAT CHEESE

MAKES ABOUT 1½ CUPS

8 ounces goat cheese, at room temperature

6 tablespoons heavy (whipping) cream

1 teaspoon minced olive-oil-preserved black truffles

Kosher salt and pepper

Combine the goat cheese, cream, and truffles in a stand mixer fitted with the whisk attachment. Whip on high speed until fluffy in texture. Season to taste with salt and pepper. Store airtight in the refrigerator for up to 2 weeks.

SOUS-VIDE CHICKEN LIVER PÂTÉ

MAKES 5 SERVINGS

1 pound chicken livers, trimmed of fat

2 cups buttermilk

4 slices bacon, roughly chopped

1 onion, diced

1 shallot, minced

1 clove garlic, smashed

1 cup sweet vermouth (I use Carpano Antica)

½ teaspoon fresh thyme

1 bay leaf

¼ teaspoon curing salt

4 eggs

1 egg yolk

½ teaspoon kosher salt

½ teaspoon black pepper

2 sticks (8 ounces) salted butter, melted

1 Soak the chicken livers in a bowl with the buttermilk for at least 2 hours. Discard the buttermilk.

2 Set your sous-vide water bath to 154°F using your immersion circulator.

3 Put the bacon in a cast-iron pan and cook over medium heat, stirring occasionally. As the bacon fat begins to render, add the onion, shallot, and garlic. Sauté until translucent and remove from the heat. Stir in the vermouth, thyme, and bay leaf, and allow to cool for 20 minutes, so that all the flavors can meld.

4 Strain the liquid through a chinois or a fine-mesh sieve and into a blender. Make sure to squeeze out as much liquid as possible. Add the chicken livers, curing salt, whole eggs, egg yolk, salt, and pepper. Blend the mixture until completely smooth. As the puree blends, slowly pour in the melted butter, as if making mayo. Once emulsified, pour the mixture again through a chinois or a fine-mesh sieve for a smooth texture. You'll have to work fast as the mixture will oxidize and brown the longer it's exposed to air. Pour the strained mixture into five ½-pint canning jars.

5 Seal the jars, place in the heated water bath, and cook for 1 hour 30 minutes. Toward the end of the cooking time, prepare an ice bath (a bowl of ice and water). Transfer the canning jars to the ice bath to cool for a few minutes, then refrigerate. The pâté should be completely chilled before serving.

DEMI-GLACE

MAKES ABOUT 1½ CUPS

5½ cups beef stock

⅔ cup red wine

1 teaspoon MSG

½ teaspoon sugar

½ teaspoon kosher salt

4 dried porcini mushrooms

Combine the beef stock, red wine, MSG, sugar, salt, and mushrooms in a large heavy-bottomed pot and bring to a simmer over medium heat. Cook to reduce the liquid by half. Strain the liquid and return it to medium heat. Discard the mushrooms. Cook to reduce by half again. Serve immediately. Refrigerate for up to 2 weeks.

TRUFFLED DEMI-GLACE: Just before using, stir in 1 tablespoon sliced black truffles packed in olive oil.

BOOZY CHEESE SAUCE

MAKES ABOUT 5 CUPS

"Boozy cheese sauce" pretty much sums up my game on every first date I've ever been on. This crowd-pleaser is super simple—because science.

½ cup cold beer or wine
13 grams sodium citrate*
6 cups sharp white cheddar, shredded

You can find this emulsifier online.

Combine the booze of your choice with the sodium citrate in a small heavy-bottomed saucepan and bring to a simmer. Stir the mixture until the sodium citrate dissolves, then add the shredded cheese. Continue to stir the sauce until the cheese has completely melted, about 2 minutes. Use an immersion blender to obtain a smooth texture. Serve hot, on everything.

IPA CHEDDAR CHEESE SAUCE: For this sauce (used in the Pickleback stack, page 46), I use a nice hoppy IPA for the "booze."

RIESLING CHEDDAR CHEESE SAUCE: I use a dry Riesling in this sauce, which goes on the Hawaiian Five "O" Face burger (page 57).

PARMESAN MORNAY

MAKES ABOUT 1 QUART

4 cups whole milk
½ yellow onion
1 bay leaf
4 tablespoons salted butter
¼ cup all-purpose flour
1¼ cups shredded Parmesan cheese
    Kosher salt and black pepper
    Freshly grated nutmeg

1 Combine the milk, onion, and bay leaf in a heavy-bottomed saucepan. Bring to a gradual simmer over low heat, stirring occasionally to prevent scorching. Once the milk begins to bubble, remove from the heat. Let the onion and bay leaf sit in the milk for at least 20 minutes, and then remove with tongs.

2 Meanwhile, melt the butter in a cast-iron or heavy-bottomed pan over medium heat. Stir in the flour until smooth to make a roux. Cook the roux until it's pale gold in color and starts to have an almost nutty aroma, about 7 minutes.

3 Whisk the warm milk into the roux until fully incorporated, to make a béchamel. Bring the béchamel to a simmer over medium heat, stirring frequently. When the sauce begins to bubble, whisk in the Parmesan until melted. Season to taste with salt and pepper and a pinch of freshly grated nutmeg. Keep warm until ready to serve.

CREAMY HUNTER SAUCE (SAUCE CHASSEUR)

MAKES ABOUT 4 SERVINGS (½ CUP)

2 tablespoons butter

1 onion, diced

1 cup sliced mushrooms

½ cup red wine

½ cup Demi-Glace (page 186)

1 medium tomato, diced

1 tablespoon heavy cream

2 tablespoons chopped fresh parsley

Melt the butter in a cast-iron pan over medium heat. Add the onion and mushrooms and sauté until the onion is translucent. Add the red wine and simmer until the wine reduces by half, about 4 minutes. Stir in the demi-glace and tomato and cook to reduce by half. Stir in the heavy cream and parsley. Serve warm.

PINEAPPLE GASTRIQUE

MAKES ½ CUP

The gastrique is an often underrated sauce. I like to think of it as the French equivalent of a sweet-and-sour sauce. (Think duck à l'orange.) This one, in particular, goes especially well with game fowl and all things pork.

3 tablespoons sugar

2 tablespoons rice vinegar

1½ cups chicken stock

1 cup fresh pineapple juice

2 dried Thai red chiles

Heat the sugar in a medium-size, heavy-bottomed pan over medium heat. Let the sugar sit untouched as it dissolves and turns dark amber in color, about 5 minutes. Gradually add the vinegar, stirring constantly until the caramel mixture melts once again. Add the chicken stock, pineapple juice, and chiles, and bring to a simmer. Let the gastrique reduce until there's only about half a cup of liquid remaining. It should have a light syrup consistency and easily coat the back of a spoon. Discard the chiles and store the gastrique in an airtight container in the refrigerator for up to 3 weeks. This can be made up to 3 days in advance.

ROASTED TOMATILLO SALSA

MAKES 1 HEAPING CUP

7 medium tomatillos, husks on

1 jalapeño, halved, seeds removed

¼ cup fresh lime juice (about 2 limes)

⅓ cup roughly chopped fresh cilantro

Kosher salt

1 Preheat the oven to 375°F.

2 Place the tomatillos on a baking sheet, stemmed side down, and roast until the juices start to leak from their husks, 20 to 30 minutes. Remove from the oven and allow to cool.

3 Once you can handle the tomatillos with your bare hands, remove their husks over a food processor, using a knife at the stem end if needed, and drop the tomatillos in. Add the jalapeño, lime juice, and cilantro and pulse until you get the texture you want, chunky or smooth. Season with salt to taste. Store airtight in the refrigerator for up to 1 week.

CAFFEINATED MAPLE SYRUP

MAKES 1 CUP

¼ cup ground dark-roast coffee

1 cup pure maple syrup, warmed*

* The warmer the syrup, the easier it will be to steep.

Combine the coffee grounds and warm maple syrup in a small container and allow to steep for 5 minutes, then strain. Store in an airtight container.

CHORIZO HOLLANDAISE

MAKES ABOUT 1 CUP

2 links fresh chorizo sausage, casings removed

½ cup butter

4 egg yolks

½ lemon, juiced

Black pepper

Tabasco sauce (optional)

1 Cook the chorizo in the butter in a skillet over medium heat, breaking up the sausage with a spatula and stirring with the butter until the sausage has fully cooked. Set a sieve over a bowl and drain the sausage into it. Reserve the sausage and butter.

2 Fill a small pot with about 1 inch of water and bring to a simmer. In a small bowl (that will fit over the pot but not touch the simmering water), whisk together the egg yolks and lemon juice until lightened in color, 1 to 2 minutes. Place the bowl over the simmering water, making sure the bottom of the bowl does not touch the surface, and continue whisking until the mixture is thick enough to coat the back of a spoon, 3 to 5 minutes.

3 Remove the yolk mixture from the heat. Slowly drizzle the reserved chorizo butter into the yolk mixture, whisking constantly. The sauce will thicken and double in size. If the mixture becomes too thick, simply spoon in some warm water, one spoonful at a time. Stir in the reserved sausage for texture. Season to taste with pepper and Tabasco. Serve immediately or keep in a warm place until ready to serve.

SAUSAGE GRAVY

MAKES ABOUT 1 QUART

Having grown up eating a lot of Southern food, I find sausage gravy to be one of life's greatest pleasures. I'll be the first to admit that my own version is slightly bastardized. I've added mushrooms, which when diced add a nice texture and additional umami. Make no mistake, this recipe makes an obscene amount of gravy, which is exactly how I like it. The good news is it will hold for days in your refrigerator. Ladle extra gravy over Cheddar Buttermilk Biscuits (page 233), Deesnuts (page 241), Liège Waffles (page 234), or even some Beef Leaf Fries (page 263). I've been known to eat it cold out of the refrigerator, with a spoon. Have a pillow and blanket within arm's reach. There will be naps.

- 3 tablespoons butter
- 2 medium white onions, diced
- 2 cups diced mushrooms
- 1 pound sage sausage (or any breakfast pork sausage)
- ¼ teaspoon chili flakes
- 3 tablespoons all-purpose flour
- 1½ cups whole milk
- 1 tablespoon crème fraîche
  Kosher salt and black pepper

1 Melt the butter in a large cast-iron skillet over medium-high heat. Add the onions and mushrooms and sauté until the onions are translucent, about 5 minutes. Stir in the sausage and chili flakes, breaking up any chunks of sausage with a spatula as you stir. When all of the sausage has cooked through, add the flour and continue sautéing for a couple of minutes. Next, stir in the milk and crème fraîche until combined. Bring the mixture to a simmer, then remove from the heat.

2 The sausage gravy I grew up on was always slightly heavy on the pepper, which is exactly how I like it—that said, season the gravy to your own liking with salt and pepper. Serve in large dollops.

TRUFFLED SAUSAGE GRAVY: Stir 1 teaspoon minced oil-packed black truffle into the gravy just before serving.

UNI BEURRE BLANC

MAKES ABOUT 1 CUP

- ½ cup sea urchin (uni)*
- 2 sticks (8 ounces) salted butter
- ½ cup dry white wine
- ½ cup white wine vinegar
- 1 small shallot, minced
- ½ lemon, juiced
  Kosher salt

* Available at Asian grocers or from your local fishmonger

1 Puree the uni and butter together in a food processor until smooth.

2 Combine the white wine, vinegar, and shallot in a saucepan and bring to a simmer over medium heat. Reduce the liquid until there's only about 3 tablespoons left, about 10 minutes. Reduce the heat to low and while constantly stirring, whisk in 1 tablespoon of the uni butter at a time, waiting for each tablespoon to melt and emulsify before introducing another. Be careful not to let the sauce boil, or it will break. If your beurre blanc does overheat and break, simply remove the sauce from the heat and whisk in ice chips until you regain an emulsion, or stable sauce. Serve immediately or keep in a warm place until ready to serve.

PARMESAN MORNAY

SAUSAGE GRAVY

HEAVEN

CHORIZO HOLLANDAISE

UNI

VEGETABLE ACCOUTRE-MENTS

ANCHO-CHILE-RUBBED GRILLED CORN

Grilled corn is one of the easiest ways to summer right. Some recipes will have you soak the corn in salt water before grilling, but for husked corn, this actually works against plumpness. This recipe can be kerneled and served on top of a burger like the Calicornication (page 16), or eaten straight off the cob, dressed in cilantro and crumbled cotija cheese. ▪ **MAKES 4 SERVINGS**

1 Preheat a grill to medium-high heat.

2 Put the ears of corn on the grill and cook until the kernels begin to char. Rotate the corn until all sides are slightly charred, 10 to 15 minutes.

3 Remove the corn from the grill and allow to cool slightly. Cut the kernels off both cobs and transfer to a small bowl. Fold in the chile powder, lime juice, and butter until combined. Season to taste with salt and pepper. If you intend to eat your corn on the cob, butter each cob, liberally season with chile powder, squeeze with lime, and garnish with cilantro and cotija cheese. If using as a burger topping, serve warm.

2 ears of corn, husked
1 teaspoon ancho chile powder
½ lime, juiced
2 tablespoons butter
Kosher salt and black pepper
Cilantro (optional), for garnish
Cotija cheese (optional), for garnish

ROASTED BRUSSELS SPROUTS

Brussels sprouts are more than just fetal Cabbage Patch Kids, they're one of the healthiest vegetables on the planet. But MORE IMPORTANT, they're super tasty and almost impossible to fuck up. This recipe reflects my personal taste and probably a bit of my personality: salty, with a kiss of sweet and a soft punch of acid.

• MAKES 4 SERVINGS

1 Preheat the oven to 400°F. Line a baking sheet with foil.

2 Wash and trim the sprouts. You can either halve the sprouts or pull the sprouts apart into individual leaves and save the cores, too. (Note: Keeping the Brussels sprouts in halves will almost double the cooking time.) Transfer the leaves and cores to a large bowl.

3 Add the olive oil, soy sauce, maple syrup, vinegar, fish sauce, garlic, chili flakes, and salt and pepper to taste and toss together until combined.

4 Spread the mixture on the baking sheet and roast until browned and crispy, 15 to 20 minutes (40 to 50 minutes as halves), stirring the Brussels sprouts with tongs after 10 minutes (or 20 minutes if halved).

1 pound Brussels sprouts, halved

1 tablespoon extra-virgin olive oil

2 teaspoons soy sauce

1 tablespoon pure maple syrup

1 teaspoon black vinegar or balsamic vinegar

1 teaspoon fish sauce

1 clove garlic, minced

¼ teaspoon chili flakes

Kosher salt and black pepper

CRISPY ASPARAGUS SHAVINGS

This tasty incarnation of asparagus couldn't get any easier. ▪ **MAKES 4 SERVINGS**

1 In a deep fryer or a deep heavy-bottomed pan with at least 2 inches of oil, preheat your fry oil to 350°F.

2 Using a vegetable peeler, slice the asparagus down in nice long, thin strands, until you can peel no further. Drop the asparagus strands in the hot oil and fry until crispy, 30 to 60 seconds. This can be done in batches if need be. Remove from the oil and drain. Season with the lemon zest and salt and pepper to taste.

Vegetable oil, for frying
1 bunch asparagus
Grated zest of 1 lemon
Kosher salt and black pepper

CARAMELIZED ONIONS

Low and slow is the name of this game. All in all, these babies should take about 45 minutes of gentle sautéing to render into their fully caramelized incarnation. ▪ **MAKES ABOUT ½ CUP**

1 Combine the butter and oil in a cast-iron skillet or heavy-bottomed pan over low heat. Once the butter has melted, add the onions, stirring until the onions begin to sweat and lose moisture. Continue stirring regularly until the onions are a rich brown color. As the onions' natural sugars begin to caramelize, you'll have to stir more frequently to prevent burning.

2 Season to taste with salt. Deglaze the pan by adding the beef stock (and Worcestershire sauce if using) and stirring any browned bits that might be stuck to the bottom. Remove from the heat and season to taste with salt and pepper. These onions will hold in the refrigerator for a couple of weeks. Simply reheat before serving.

1 tablespoon butter

2 tablespoons grapeseed oil

2 yellow onions, cut into ⅛-inch-thick slices

Kosher salt

2 tablespoons beef stock or red wine

1 teaspoon Worcestershire sauce (optional)

Black pepper

BLACK-VINEGAR-MARINATED ONIONS

Black vinegar holds the personal distinction of being the only vinegar I've ever considered wearing dabbed behind my ears as a cologne. Woody, slightly malty, with a dark molasses richness, black vinegar is as complex as it is bold. Soaking onions in this elixir cuts their bite and enhances their intrigue, making them the perfect secret weapon. ▪ **MAKES ABOUT 2 CUPS**

1 Marinate the sliced raw onions in the black vinegar for a couple of hours before serving. Toss the onions occasionally as they soak.

2 When you're ready to serve, drain the onions and sauté them with a drizzle of olive oil in a skillet over medium heat, until they're soft and begin to sweeten, about 5 minutes.

2 onions, halved and cut into
¼-inch-thick half-moons
1 cup black vinegar
Extra-virgin olive oil, for the pan

SHALLOT/ONION/GARLIC CONFIT

A confit sounds fancy, but it simply means cooking something submerged in fat. Originally, the technique was utilized primarily as a method of preservation for proteins like duck or pork. Cooked and stored in their own fat, they could be kept at room temperature for long periods without fear of spoilage. For aromatics like shallot, onion, or even garlic, this method is a super-easy way to render them sweet and tender. Better yet, their savory flavors infuse the very oil they're cooked in, which can be used for drizzling over cooked meats, tossing with roast vegetables, brushing on toast, or even mixing into salad dressings.

1 Preheat the oven to 350°F.

2 Place sliced onions or shallots, or whole peeled garlic cloves, in a baking dish and submerge in extra-virgin olive oil. I usually add a couple sprigs of fresh thyme or a bay leaf for extra flavor. Bake for about 45 minutes.

3 Store together, or strain and store separately, in the refrigerator for about 1 week.

CREAMED CORN

Depending on where you grew up, you may also know this dish as "Wet Dreamed Corn." While the canned stuff might exemplify the culinary peak of the canned vegetable era, there's nothing like the real deal. This dish plays well on burgers, bacon-wrapped hot dogs, and, of course, as a side at holiday feastings. ▪ **MAKES 3 CUPS**

1 Cut the kernels from the corncobs with a sharp knife and place in a bowl. Then run the back side of the knife over the cut cobs to push out the corn milk into the bowl.

2 Melt the bacon grease in a medium cast-iron skillet or heavy-bottomed pan over medium heat. Add the shallot, garlic, and roughly half of the corn. Sweat the vegetables until the shallots have softened, about 5 minutes. Gently stir in the flour until combined. Add the buttermilk and chicken stock and bring to a simmer. Cook until thickened, about 10 minutes, stirring occasionally to prevent it from scorching. Transfer the mixture to a blender or food processor and pulse a few times to a consistency just above puree.

3 Return the corn mixture to the same skillet and fold in the remaining corn kernels, the sugar, sour cream, and thyme. Bring the creamed corn to a gentle simmer and cook over medium heat for 10 minutes. If the mixture becomes too thick, stir in more chicken stock 1 tablespoon at a time. Season to taste with salt and pepper. Serve warm or store in the refrigerator for up to a few days.

5 ears of corn

1 tablespoon bacon grease or butter

1 small shallot, diced

2 cloves garlic, minced

1 tablespoon all-purpose flour

1 cup buttermilk

1/2 cup chicken stock

1 teaspoon sugar

2 tablespoons sour cream

Leaves from 3 or 4 sprigs thyme, minced

Kosher salt and black pepper

COLD-SMOKED TOMATOES

I'm a total toma-hoe. These cold-smoked tomatoes are nice for beefing up burgers but can also add some unexpected play to, say, a caprese salad. ▪ **MAKES 4 SERVINGS**

Place your tomato slices in an airtight container. Using a smoking gun,* fill the container with smoke and seal. Let the tomato sit for 15 minutes before unsealing. Serve immediately.

1 tomato, sliced
1 tablespoon hickory wood chips

* *While I highly recommend getting a smoking gun, if you don't have one you can always MacGyver your own method for smoking. Like for Smoked Trout (page 154), you'll need a large pot, a steamer insert, and some foil. Put a layer of foil on the bottom of the pot. Add wood chips and cover with another layer of foil. Place the steamer insert on top, followed by the tomato slices. Heat the wood chips over medium-high heat until they begin smoking, then quickly seal the top of the pot with a tight wrapping of foil and remove from the heat. Proceed as in the smoking gun instructions.*

OLD BAY AND BACON POTATO SALAD

This salad houses all of my favorite baes—Old Bae and baecon!—in one place. If you're serving this dish as a stand-alone, I recommend topping it with a heaping spoonful of smoked trout roe. The smoky bursts of salty brine will make you an instant hero, if only in your own mind. ▪ **MAKE 4 TO 6 SERVINGS**

1 Place the potatoes in a large saucepan and cover with cold water. Season the water with salt until it's salty like the sea. Bring the pot to a boil and simmer until the potatoes are fork-tender, about 30 minutes. Drain the potatoes, allow to cool, cut into bite-size pieces, and place in a large bowl.

2 Add the celery, shallot, mustard, mayo, sambal, Old Bay, bacon, and tomatoes and toss until combined. Refrigerate for at least 1 hour before serving. The longer the potato salad sits in the refrigerator, the more the flavors will meld. This can be made 1 day in advance.

1¼ pounds small waxy (boiling) potatoes

Kosher salt

1 stalk celery, diced

½ small shallot, diced (1 clove)

2 tablespoons coarse ground mustard

2 tablespoons homemade mayonnaise (page 166)

1 teaspoon sambal chili paste

½ teaspoon Old Bay seasoning

3 slices bacon, crisp-cooked and roughly chopped

6 cherry tomatoes, quartered

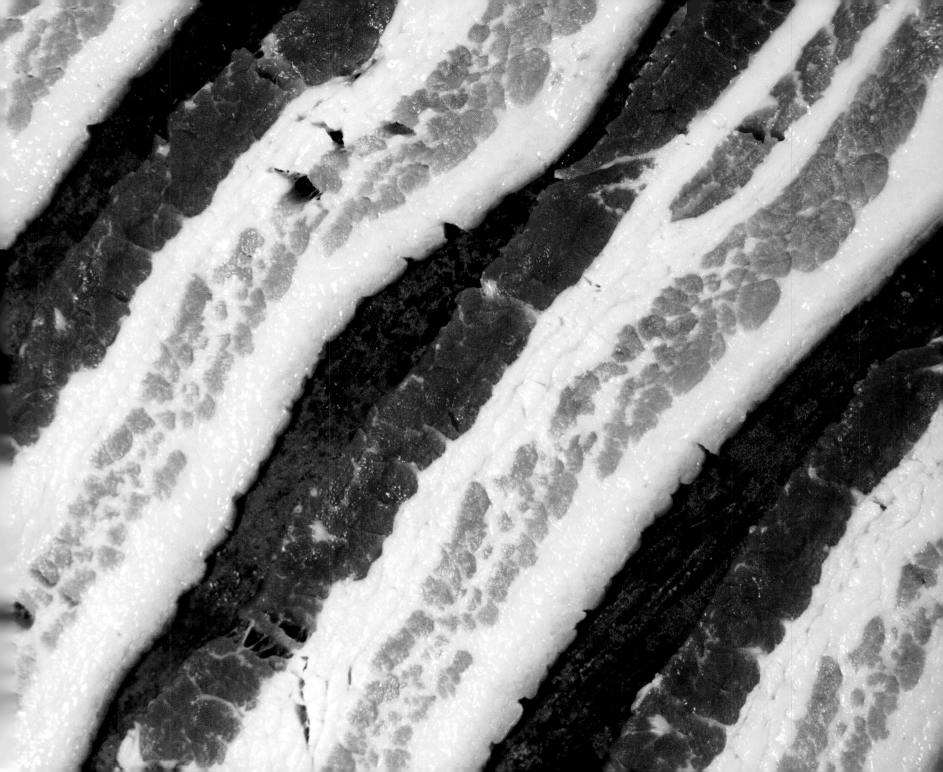

POTATO PARSNIP GRATIN

Parsnips are a natural fit for this creamy comfort dish. Earthy sweet and mild, the root vegetable adds a subtle complexity to the traditional potato palate, making this gratin the perfect companion for all things cozy.

- **MAKES 5 SERVINGS**

1 Preheat the oven to 375°F. Grease 5 cups of a hamburger bun tin.

2 Set up a bowl of ice and water. Cut the potatoes into ¼-inch-thick slices and place in the ice bath to soak. Set aside.

3 Combine the onion, garlic, cream, salt, pepper, and nutmeg in a heavy-bottomed saucepot. Bring to a gradual simmer over low heat, stirring with a silicone spatula to prevent scorching. When the cream begins to bubble, remove from the heat and pour through a fine-mesh sieve. Return the strained cream to low heat and stir in the Gruyère until melted. Remove the sauce from the heat.

4 Drain the potato slices. Arrange and alternately layer the potato and parsnip slices into each cup of the hamburger bun tin, filling them almost to the top. Carefully fill each cup with the cream sauce until flush with the top layer. Evenly distribute the Parmesan among the cups.

5 Bake until the potatoes are fork-tender and the tops are golden brown, about 40 minutes. Allow the pan to rest for 30 minutes before serving, so the gratins can set.

2 medium russet (baking) potatoes, peeled
1 onion, sliced into rings
1 clove garlic, minced
2½ cups heavy (whipping) cream
1 teaspoon kosher salt
½ teaspoon black pepper
¼ teaspoon freshly grated nutmeg
½ cup shredded Gruyère cheese
4 parsnips, cut into ¼-inch-thick slices
½ cup shredded Parmesan cheese

SMOKED SHIITAKE BACON

These fungi crisps with their smoky umami and salty crunch make me purr like a fat cat. Moreover, they're great on both veggie and carnivore burgers alike. ▪ **MAKES 4 TO 6 SERVINGS**

1 Preheat the oven to 350°F. Line a baking sheet with foil.

2 Toss the mushrooms in a medium bowl with the olive oil, fish sauce, sesame oil, sage, brown sugar, garlic powder, paprika, salt, and pepper. (If you do not have a stovetop smoker or a smoking gun, add the liquid smoke, too.) Allow the mushrooms to marinate for 30 minutes.

3 Spread the mushrooms on the baking sheet and bake for 10 minutes, flip, and then bake for an additional 10 to 15 minutes, or until crispy and nicely browned. The darker they get, the richer the flavor gets.

4 If you have a smoking gun, or a stovetop smoker, seal the crispy mushrooms in cold smoke for at least 10 minutes. Serve warm.

4 ounces shiitake mushrooms, stems discarded, caps cut into 1/8-inch-wide strips

3 tablespoons extra-virgin olive oil

1/2 teaspoon fish sauce (optional for vegetarian purposes)

1/2 teaspoon sesame oil

1 teaspoon minced fresh sage

1/2 teaspoon light brown sugar

1/4 teaspoon garlic powder

1/4 teaspoon smoked sweet paprika

1/4 teaspoon kosher salt

1/4 teaspoon black pepper

1/2 teaspoon liquid smoke or 1 tablespoon hickory or applewood smoking chips

QUICK PICKLES

QUICK PICKLED BEETS

MAKES 1 PINT

- 1 pound red beets (about 6 small)
- ½ cup red wine vinegar
- ½ cup balsamic vinegar
- 3 tablespoons sugar
- 2 teaspoons Worcestershire sauce
- 1 teaspoon kosher salt
- ¼ teaspoon cayenne pepper
- 1 bay leaf
- 10 black peppercorns

1 Throw the beets into a large pot and submerge in cold water. Bring to a simmer and cook until tender, 30 to 40 minutes. Allow the beets to cool; then they will peel with ease if you rub the skins off with a paper towel. Cut the skinned beets into skinny round slices (about ¼ inch thick) and place in a sealable heatproof pint container.

2 Combine the vinegars, sugar, Worcestershire sauce, salt, cayenne, bay leaf, and peppercorns in a small saucepan and bring to a boil. Pour the brine directly into the container with the beets and seal. Allow to cool and then refrigerate for at least 3 hours before serving. They will keep for up to 2 weeks.

QUICK PICKLED HAMBURGER DILLS

MAKES 1 PINT

- 2 Persian (mini) cucumbers, cut into ¼-inch-thick rounds
- 2 cloves garlic, peeled
- ½ shallot, peeled
- 1 tablespoon dill seeds
- 1 teaspoon caraway seeds
- 1 teaspoon mustard seeds
- 1 teaspoon coriander seeds
- ½ teaspoon chipotle chili flakes (optional)
- ½ teaspoon black peppercorns
- ¾ cup distilled white vinegar
- ¼ cup water
- 1 teaspoon sugar
- 1 teaspoon kosher salt

1 Put the cucumbers, garlic, shallot, all the seeds, the chipotle flakes (if using), and peppercorns in a 1-pint canning jar.

2 Combine the vinegar, water, sugar, and salt in a small saucepan and bring to a simmer. Pour the hot brine into the jar and screw on the lid fingertip tight. Allow to cool, then refrigerate for at least 12 hours before serving. They will keep for up to 2 weeks.

RICE VINEGAR CUCUMBER PICKLES

MAKES 1 PINT

- 2 Persian (mini) cucumbers, cut into ¼-inch-thick rounds
- 1 clove garlic, peeled
- 1 teaspoon sesame seeds, toasted (see page 219)
- ½ cup rice vinegar
- ¾ cup water
- 1 teaspoon Szechuan peppercorns*
- 3 tablespoons sugar
- 1 teaspoon kosher salt

Available at spice stores or online

1 Put the cucumbers, garlic, and sesame seeds in a 1-pint canning jar.

2 Combine the vinegar, water, peppercorns, sugar, and salt in a small saucepan and bring to a simmer. Pour the hot brine into the canning jar and seal fingertip tight. Allow to cool, then refrigerate for at least 12 hours before serving. They will keep for up to 2 weeks.

PORNBURGER QUICKIE:

GARLIC, WHY SO BLUE?

So your pickled garlic just blue itself. . . . No biggie; it's totally natural and, more important, perfectly safe. When garlic sits in acid, such as vinegar, the cell membranes of the clove rupture, resulting in a chemical romance between the garlic's amino acids and sulfur compounds. In fact, in Northern China, a greenish blue pickled garlic (or Laba garlic) is celebrated as a New Year's delicacy.

QUICK PICKLED HAMBURGER DILLS

RED ONION PICKLES

PICKLED FENNEL

RED CABBAGE SLAW

JALAPEÑO PICKLES

MAKES 1 PINT

¾ cup apple cider vinegar

½ cup water

2 tablespoons sugar

1 tablespoon kosher salt

1 teaspoon dried oregano

2 cloves garlic, peeled

7 to 10 jalapeños (the bigger they are, the less spicy), sliced into ¼-inch-thick rounds

Combine the vinegar, water, sugar, salt, oregano, and garlic in a small saucepan. Bring to a simmer, stirring the salt and sugar until they dissolve. Add the jalapeños and simmer for 1 minute before removing from the heat. Use tongs to transfer the garlic and jalapeños to a sealable pint container, and top off with the hot brine. Allow them to sit for at least a few hours and ideally a full day before serving. Store airtight in the refrigerator for up to 2 weeks.

RED ONION PICKLES

MAKES 1 PINT

1 large red onion, thinly sliced

½ teaspoon black peppercorns

1 whole star anise pod

1 cinnamon stick

1 cup sherry vinegar

1 teaspoon kosher salt

2 tablespoons sugar

1 Put the onions, peppercorns, star anise, and cinnamon in a 1-pint canning jar.

2 Combine the vinegar, salt, and sugar in a small saucepan and bring to a simmer, stirring until the salt and sugar dissolve. Fill the canning jar to the top with the hot brine. Allow the onions to pickle for 12 hours before eating. Store airtight in the refrigerator for up to 2 weeks.

RED CABBAGE SLAW

MAKES ABOUT 1 QUART

1 tablespoon sesame seeds

½ teaspoon caraway seeds

1 quart shredded red cabbage (about ½ cabbage)

1 jalapeño, seeded and minced

½ red onion, diced

2 tablespoons chopped fresh cilantro

¼ cup lime juice (about 2 limes, juiced)

2 tablespoons apple cider vinegar

1 tablespoon Sriracha sauce

1 tablespoon extra-virgin olive oil

½ teaspoon sesame oil

Kosher salt and black pepper

1 Warm a small heavy-bottomed pan over medium heat and toast the sesame and caraway seeds, shaking the pan occasionally, until the seeds darken slightly and become fragrant. Remove the seeds from the heat, as they will quickly burn.

2 Toss together the cabbage, jalapeño, onion, cilantro, sesame seeds, caraway seeds, lime juice, vinegar, Sriracha, olive oil, sesame oil, and salt and pepper to taste in a large bowl. Allow the flavors to meld in the refrigerator for at least 1 hour before serving. Store airtight in the refrigerator for up to 1 week.

PICKLED FENNEL

MAKES 1 PINT

- 1 medium bulb of fennel, sliced into thin rings
- ½ shallot (1 clove), peeled
- 1 teaspoon Szechuan peppercorns*
- 1 teaspoon coriander seeds
- 1 whole star anise pod
- Zest of 1 orange, removed with a vegetable peeler
- ¾ cup rice vinegar
- ½ cup water
- 1 teaspoon kosher salt
- 3 tablespoons sugar

Available at a spice store or online

1 Put the fennel, shallot, peppercorns, coriander seeds, star anise pod, and orange zest in a 1-pint canning jar.

2 Combine the vinegar, water, salt, and sugar in a small saucepan. Bring to a simmer, stirring until the salt and sugar dissolve. Pour the hot brine into the canning jar, filling to the top. Seal fingertip tight and allow the fennel to pickle for 24 hours in the refrigerator before eating. Store airtight in the refrigerator for up to 2 weeks.

PICKLED HOT DOGS

MAKES 1 PINT

- 8 mini hot dogs or 4 regular hot dogs
- 2 cloves garlic, peeled
- 1 shallot clove, peeled
- 1 bay leaf
- 12 allspice berries
- 12 black peppercorns
- 1 teaspoon mustard seeds
- 1 teaspoon coriander seeds
- ½ teaspoon chili flakes
- ¾ cup distilled white vinegar
- ¼ cup water
- 2 teaspoons sugar
- 1 teaspoon kosher salt

1 With a small sharp knife, butterfly-cut the mini hot dogs down the middle, leaving them attached. If using regular hot dogs, halve them crosswise, then butterfly-cut the halves. Transfer the hot dogs to a 1-pint canning jar and add the garlic, shallot, bay leaf, allspice, peppercorns, mustard seeds, coriander seeds, and chili flakes.

2 Combine the vinegar, water, sugar, and salt in a small saucepan and bring to a boil. Once the sugar and salt have dissolved, remove the pot from the heat.

3 Pour the hot brine into the canning jar and seal. Allow the pickles to brine for at least 24 hours in the refrigerator before eating. Store airtight in the refrigerator for up to 2 weeks.

PORNBURGER QUICKIE:

JUICING

Save that pickle juice! Like any good gateway drug, this magical brine can lead to bigger and better downward spirals, like Fried Chicken (page 146), the Pickleback (page 46), and even my liquid burger cocktail, the Liquid Diet (page 280).

And once you inevitably hit rock bottom? (Let's be honest, there's always a rock bottom.) The cure-all elixir can actually get you back on your feet, replenishing your depleted sodium levels of hangover hell and enabling you to ride that roller coaster on repeat like a snake eating its tail.

BUNS & BATTER

BRIOCHE BUNS

First impressions are important, which is why I let these bubble buns do the all the talking. Buttery with supple squish and subtle sweetness . . . these babies got all the back. ▪ **MAKES 12 BUNS**

1 Combine the yeast, water, milk, and sugar in a small bowl. Allow the yeast to activate and foam for roughly 5 minutes.

2 Beat the 4 eggs in another small bowl until combined.

3 In the bowl of a stand mixer fitted with a paddle attachment, combine the flour, salt, and butter. Mix on medium speed until the butter and flour have a "crumby" texture.

4 Add the yeast mixture and beaten eggs to the flour. Mix the ingredients (still with the paddle attachment) for about 10 minutes on low. The dough at this point should be incredibly slack and sticky. You want to be able to hold the dough and allow it to drop to the counter without breaking.

5 Using as little additional flour as possible, shape the dough into a ball and set it in a greased bowl. Cover with a dampened kitchen towel and allow the dough to rise in a warm spot until it has doubled in size. It should take anywhere from 1 to 3 hours to double. Remember, it's about size, not time.

6 Dusting your hands with flour, gently punch down the dough to remove air bubbles and portion the dough into 8 equal pieces. (I like to use a scale for precision and to ensure equal cooking time.) Again, the less flour used for shaping and handling, the better.

7 Line a baking sheet with parchment paper. Take each piece of dough and flatten it with the palm of your hand to form a disc. Fold over each of the four sides and pinch in the middle.

4½ teaspoons active dry yeast

½ cup warm water (105°F to 110°F)

3 tablespoons warm milk (105°F to 110°F)

3 tablespoons sugar

4 large eggs

3 cups plus 3 tablespoons bread flour*

2 teaspoons kosher salt

10 tablespoons salted butter, at room temperature

Egg wash: 1 egg beaten with a splash of water

*Bread flour has more gluten than all-purpose flour and allows for better structure. It can be found at your local grocery or online.

Flip the dough so that the seam side is down and use your palm to gently roll the dough into a smooth ball, resembling a bun. Place the shaped dough on the lined baking sheet, leaving 2 to 3 inches between buns. Loosely cover the buns with plastic wrap and allow them to rise for roughly another hour. They should be nice and puffy.

8 Meanwhile, preheat the oven to 400°F.

9 Using a pastry brush, give the buns a nice gloss of egg wash. Place an ovenproof bowl with 1 cup water on the bottom shelf of the oven. This will give you the steam you need to get a nice and subtle crunch in the crust. Place your baking sheet of buns on the top shelf uncovered and bake until golden brown, 14 to 16 minutes. Allow to cool completely on a wire rack.

SESAME BRIOCHE BUNS: Sprinkle ⅓ cup sesame seeds over the buns right after you brush them with the egg wash.

CHEESEBURGER POP TARTS

I gave up on trying to hang out with these pop tarts a long time ago. . . . Turns out, they're flaky as fuck. Wink. ▪ **MAKES 6**

1 Make the pastry: Combine the flour, salt, and sugar in a medium bowl and whisk together. Using a fork, blend the butter into the mixture until it resembles a coarse meal. Mix in the ice water 1 tablespoon at a time and form the dough into a ball. Divide the ball in two, wrap in plastic, and refrigerate for about 1 hour.

2 Roll out each of the dough balls on a well-floured surface until they're both roughly ⅛ inch thick. Using a pastry cutter or a sharp knife, cut the dough into 4 x 6-inch rectangles. You should be able to make at least 12 rectangles at this size. Reroll scraps if necessary to get more.

3 For the filling and to assemble the pop tarts: Designate half of the rectangles as pop tart "tops" and the others as "bottoms." Spread about 1 tablespoon bacon jam on each of the bottoms, leaving at least a ½-inch border around the edges. Next—and this is going to sound weird—roll out your ground beef on a washable cutting board until it's ¼ inch thick. Using a metal spatula, portion and place the beef equally to stack on the bottoms, maintaining the ½-inch border. Sprinkle each portion of beef with a good pinch of minced shallot. Top each portion with 6 slices of the hamburger dills, as well as 1 slice of cheese.

4 And now to seal the deal: Cover the stacks with the dough tops. Use your fingertips to firmly seal the edges by pinching them shut, then imprint the edges with the tines of a fork to make a crimp pattern. Place the sealed pop tarts on a baking sheet lined with parchment paper and freeze for at least 1 hour. The uncooked pop tarts can be made days or weeks in advance, and frozen for when your pop tart cravings attack.

5 When ready to serve, preheat the oven to 450°F. Brush the pop tarts with egg wash and sprinkle with sesame seeds.

6 Bake the pop tarts until the pastry starts to brown, about 15 minutes. Allow to cool for a few minutes before plating. Serve with smoky burger sauce for dipping.

PASTRY:

- 2 cups all-purpose flour, plus more for rolling
- 1 teaspoon kosher salt
- 1 teaspoon sugar
- 2 sticks (8 ounces) cold salted butter, cut into ½-inch pieces
- 6 tablespoons ice water

FILLING:

- 6 tablespoons Bacon Jam (page 181)
- 1 pound PornBurger blend (page 91)
- 1 shallot, minced
- 1 large jar hamburger dills
- 6 American cheese slices

Egg wash: 1 egg beaten with a splash of water

Sesame seeds, for garnish

PornBurger Smoky Burger Sauce (page 166), for serving

PORNBURGER QUICKIE:

WHITE CASTLE

Anybody who knows me knows that one of my greatest/guiltiest pleasures on earth is inhaling a White Castle cheeseburger, and then a few more. Seriously, it's a problem. A legend by any standard, White Castle holds a very unique place in history. Not only did it have THE original slider, it's also lauded as the first fast-food burger chain ever . . . that's EVER! On top of that, its bite-size "square-don't-care" patties are literally engineered for speed. Steamed on a bed of rehydrated onions, each patty has been systematically bored with five holes for rapid steam-cooked seduction. Forget the "one flip" argument—these patties are flipped exactly zero times, with zero fucks given. Coincidentally, it's this unique steam-cooked method that makes these sliders a perfect candidate for the microwave as well. Don't live near a location? No problem. They're available at most supermarkets, in the frozen food section. Pickles not included.

WHITE CASTLE CHEESEBURGER WAFFLES

The force is strong with these waffled White Castles, but then again I'm easily biased when two of my favorite things come packaged together. (Amiright pot brownies?!) Plus, these burger buns come with built-in handholds, making it EVEN EASIER to fully embrace your dark side. ▪ **MAKES 8 "WAFFLES"**

Preheat a waffle iron and coat it with cooking spray. Microwave the frozen cheeseburgers as directed on the box—I cook them for 1 minute per two-pack. Remove the cooked cheeseburgers from their packaging and place in the middle of the waffle iron and press shut. Cook until golden delicious, about 2 minutes.

8 frozen White Castle cheeseburgers (see page 229)

CHEDDAR BUTTERMILK BISCUITS

The only thing more American than flexing these bad boys around the breakfast table, is stuffing them with a burger and smothering them with sausage gravy. To avoid flaccid biscuits, make sure you keep your dough thoroughly chilled throughout the mixing process. That said, a little Marvin Gaye on the stereo never hurt either. ▪ **MAKES 8 BISCUITS**

1 Preheat the oven to 500°F. Line a baking sheet with parchment paper or a silicone baking mat.

2 Combine the flour, cornmeal, baking powder, cayenne, salt, and sugar in a food processor. Pulse the cubed butter together with the flour mixture a couple times, leaving sizable chunks of butter. Add the shredded cheese and pulse a couple more times.

3 In a small bowl, whisk together the egg and the buttermilk. Combine the buttermilk and flour mixture into a large bowl, and use your hands to incorporate all the ingredients into a semi-sticky dough. Let the dough rest in the refrigerator for 30 minutes.

4 Turn the dough out onto a lightly floured surface and roll into a rectangle, roughly ½ inch thick. Fold each side of the dough toward the center, so that both ends meet in the middle and the dough becomes more of a square. Fold the dough in half, like a book, and repeat the laminating process an additional two times. Lightly dust with flour, as needed. Place the folded dough in the refrigerator and allow to rest for 15 minutes.

5 In a small bowl, combine the egg yolk with the water to make an egg wash. Roll the dough out once more, so that it's about ½ inch thick. Use a 4-inch round cutter to shape the biscuits. Place the biscuits on the baking sheet, brush the tops with the egg wash, and bake until they're golden brown, 11 to 14 minutes. Allow them to rest for at least 5 minutes before serving.

1¾ cups all-purpose flour
¼ cup yellow cornmeal
1 tablespoon plus 2 teaspoons baking powder
1 teaspoon garlic powder
¼ teaspoon cayenne pepper
½ teaspoon salt
1 teaspoon sugar
1½ sticks (6 ounces) butter, chilled and cubed
1¼ cups shredded cheddar cheese
1 egg, beaten
1 cup cold buttermilk
1 egg yolk
1 tablespoon water

LIÈGE WAFFLES

In the fiefdom that is waffles, the Liège reigns supreme. Rather than the product of a super-wet batter, these Belgian-style waffles are yeast-risen, much like bread. And while they take some time to make, the steps are easy and the result is out of this world. ▪ **MAKES 8 WAFFLES**

1 In a stand mixer fitted with a dough hook, combine the buttermilk, yeast, brown sugar, and water. Stir just enough to combine and let the yeast sit until it gets foamy, about 5 minutes.

2 Stir in the eggs, honey, vanilla, salt, granulated sugar, and butter. Mix until incorporated. Add the flour 1 cup at a time, and knead the mixture on a lightly floured surface until the dough forms and is smooth and slightly sticky in consistency, about 5 minutes. If the dough is too wet, add more flour, 1 tablespoon at a time, until you get a smoother dough.

3 Place the dough in a greased bowl. Cover with a dampened kitchen towel and allow the dough to rise in a warm spot until it has more than doubled in size, about 3 hours.

4 Punch down the dough and transfer it back to the bowl. Cover tightly with plastic wrap and refrigerate overnight (or at least 8 hours).

5 Preheat your waffle iron on its lowest setting. Remove the firmed dough from the fridge and knead the pearl sugar into the dough. Roll the dough into a log and divide it into 8 equal pieces.

6 Grease your waffle iron and place a piece of the portioned dough in the middle. Cook until golden brown, 3 to 5 minutes. Continue with the rest of the dough. Serve hot.

½ cup buttermilk, heated to lukewarm (105°F to 110°F)

1 tablespoon active dry yeast

2 teaspoons light brown sugar

⅓ cup warm water (105°F to 110°F)

2 large eggs, beaten, at room temperature

2 tablespoons honey

1 tablespoon plus 1 teaspoon vanilla

1 teaspoon kosher salt

3 tablespoons granulated sugar

1 cup salted butter, at room temperature

3 cups all-purpose flour

1 cup Belgian pearl sugar*

Belgian pearl sugar can be found online or at your specialty baking store. If you don't have pearl sugar on hand, you can break up sugar cubes.

POTATO-CHIP-CRUSTED FOIE GRAS GOUGÈRES

As if these cheese puffs weren't French enough, I went ahead and added some foie gras for flavor. No foie gras? No problem. Simply substitute 2 tablespoons of butter for the foie gras. ▪ **MAKES AT LEAST 8 SLIDER BUNS**

1 Preheat the oven to 350°F.

2 Combine the butter and foie gras in a small baking dish and bake until soft, about 10 minutes. Transfer the mixture to a blender and puree.

3 Transfer the puree to a medium saucepan, add the milk, and bring to a simmer. Add the salt, nutmeg, and flour and stir with a wooden spoon over medium heat until combined. The dough should start to pull away from the edges and form a ball after a couple of minutes. Continue stirring until the dough is no longer sticky and a layer of film develops on the bottom of the pan, 2 to 3 minutes longer. Remove the pan from the heat and slowly stir in the eggs, until fully combined. Stir in the cheeses.

4 Increase the oven to 425°F. Line a baking sheet with parchment paper. Use a greased hemispherical (round) tablespoon measure to measure out each gougère—2 stacked tablespoons of dough for each—and arrange on the baking sheet, leaving a couple of inches between them because they puff up while baking.

5 Bake the gougères for 15 minutes. As they bake, combine the cornstarch dissolved in cold water and the boiling water in a bowl to create a glaze. After 15 minutes, remove the gougères from the oven and quickly brush each one with the glaze, followed by a sprinkle of crumbled potato chips. Put the gougères back in the oven and cook until golden brown, about 15 minutes longer.

4 tablespoons butter

2 ounces foie gras, cut roughly into cubes

½ cup whole milk

½ teaspoon kosher salt

Pinch of freshly grated nutmeg

1¼ cups all-purpose flour

4 eggs, beaten

3 ounces Gruyère cheese, grated (about ¾ cup)*

3 ounces Parmesan cheese, grated (about ¾ cup)*

2 tablespoons cornstarch, dissolved in ¼ cup cold water

1 cup boiling water

1 small package crumbled potato chips

I weigh out my cheese when baking for better precision. Cup measurements can vary depending on the size of the grating holes.

RICE BUNS

Rice "buns," as popularized by the Japanese chain MOS Burger, are a fun alternative to bread as usual. While they do have a tendency to break down structurally, a well-placed burger wrapper or folded parchment paper is an easy hack that will make you an instant pro. ▪ **MAKES ENOUGH FOR 8 INDIVIDUAL BUNS (4 BURGERS)**

1 Combine the rice and water in a pot and bring to a boil, then reduce the heat to a steady simmer and cover. Simmer the rice for 15 minutes, then remove from the heat completely. Let the rice sit covered for 10 minutes. Fluff the rice with a fork, and stir in the furikake (if using). Allow the rice to cool completely.

2 Use a ¼-cup measure to scoop out portions of rice. For shaping the patties, I use a 4-inch ring mold and build the rice buns in them to a depth of about ½ inch. Place the formed buns on a lined baking sheet and keep at room temperature until ready to toast.

3 To serve, preheat a cast-iron pan over high heat with the olive oil. Toast only one side of each rice bun, about 1 minute. Be careful how you handle the toasted buns, as they're more likely to fall apart when they're warm. Allow them to cool before serving so they become more stable.

2 cups sushi rice
2½ cups water
4 tablespoons furikake* (optional)
1 tablespoon extra-virgin olive oil

Available at Asian markets or online

DEESNUTS
(CRESCENT ROLL DONUTS)

Let me start by saying that Dominique Ansel will forever be "the man" in my book. When I originally made the Willem DaFoe-nut burger (page 68), I followed his recipe to a T—well, almost. I laminated Parmesan into the dough along the way. It is a tremendous recipe. It also takes three days—THREE DAYS. I ain't got time for that. This version, while obviously not authentic, makes a super-flaky, crispy, and flavorful inspiration in only 20 minutes. Sometimes cheaters do win. ▪ **MAKES 4 DEESNUTS**

1 In a deep fryer or a deep heavy-bottomed pan with at least 2 inches of oil, preheat your fry oil to 360°F.

2 Remove each roll of crescent dough from its tube and using your hands, pat slightly flat. Dust the dough with Parmesan and then use a rolling pin to roll each portion into a long rectangle about 4 x 18 inches and about ¼ inch thick. (If you don't have a rolling pin, a wine bottle will always work.) Liberally dust with Parmesan cheese. Fold the long rectangles in half horizontally. The dough should be about ½ inch thick. Using a 5-inch biscuit cutter, cut out 2 rounds from each rectangle. Using a 1-inch cutter (I personally use a shot glass), remove the centers of the 5-inch rounds. (Save the donut holes and dough scraps for frying and bite-size nibbling.) Cutting out the centers is crucial to how the donuts will rise, and ensures that they'll cook through.

3 Gently drop each donut into the oil and fry until golden brown, 5 to 6 minutes. Flip repeatedly to ensure that they cook evenly. Drain and allow to cool for 5 minutes before cutting into— or straight up devouring—them.

Vegetable oil, for deep-frying

Two 12-ounce tubes crescent roll dough (I use Pillsbury Grands)

Grated Parmesan cheese, for dusting (about ⅓ cup)

GOAT CHEESE BEIGNETS

Fresh yeast-risen beignets are one of life's greatest pleasures. Add a little goat cheese and these French fluffers are as enticing to the savory as they are to the sweet. ▪ **MAKES 12 BEIGNETS**

1 Combine the yeast, sugar, and warm water in a large bowl and allow the yeast to activate and begin foaming, about 5 minutes. Add the eggs, buttermilk, goat cheese, and lard and combine. Stir in the flour and salt to create a wet dough. Cover the dough with plastic wrap and allow to rest overnight in the fridge. It should double in size.

2 In a deep fryer or a deep heavy-bottomed pan with at least 2 inches of oil, preheat your fry oil to 360°F.

3 Punch down the beignet dough on a floured surface and roll it out to about ¼ inch thick. Add flour as needed, but the less you use, the better. Use a pizza cutter to cut the dough into roughly 3-inch squares. Fry each square until puffed and golden brown, 5 to 6 minutes. Dust with powdered sugar and black pepper.

2¼ teaspoons active dry yeast
1 tablespoon sugar
1½ cups warm water (105°F to 110°F)
2 eggs, lightly beaten
1 cup buttermilk
4 ounces goat cheese
¼ cup lard or shortening
3 cups all-purpose flour, plus more for dusting
1 teaspoon kosher salt
Canola oil, for deep-frying
Powdered sugar, for dusting
Fresh cracked black pepper, for dusting

FRIED MACARONI AND CHEESE BUNS

Just to set the record straight, these seductive sirens are not buns. . . . They're the beckoning finger of Burger Perversion saying, "Come hither, the water is warm." I don't know about you, but I LOVE warm water. . . . #YOLO

▪ MAKES 8 SERVINGS

1 Bring a large pot of water to a boil for the pasta. Salt it until it tastes like the sea. Add the macaroni and cook for about 7 minutes. The idea is to cook the pasta a little less than you usually would, because you'll finish it with the cheese. Drain the pasta and return it to the pot. Stir in the cheeses, milk, gelatin, and nutmeg and bring to a boil. Remove from the heat and allow to cool for 5 minutes.

2 Pour the macaroni and cheese into a rimmed baking sheet and spread it around evenly. Don't worry if there seems to be excess liquid; as the macaroni and cheese sets, the excess will disappear. Carefully wrap the baking sheet with plastic and refrigerate. Allow the macaroni and cheese to chill for at least 1 hour. When it's ready, you should be able to turn the pan on its side without anything moving.

3 In a deep fryer or a deep heavy-bottomed pan with at least 2 inches of oil, preheat your fry oil to 350°F.

4 Set up a frying station: Place the eggs in one small bowl and the panko in another. Remove the macaroni and cheese from the refrigerator. Using a round cutter (I recommend using a ring about 3 inches in diameter, because all that macaroni and cheese quickly adds up to an inevitable belly buster), cut out "buns." Dip the macaroni buns into the beaten egg, allowing the excess to drip off, and then into the panko, making sure to evenly coat on each side.

5 Fry the buns until golden brown, 3 to 5 minutes. Drain and serve hot.

Kosher salt

1 pound macaroni

5 ounces white cheddar cheese, grated* (about 1¼ cups)

5 ounces Gruyère cheese, grated* (about 1¼ cups)

5 ounces Parmesan cheese, grated* (about 1¼ cups)

1 cup whole milk

1 packet unflavored gelatin

2 pinches of freshly grated nutmeg
Canola oil, for deep-frying

2 eggs, beaten

1 cup panko bread crumbs

*I weigh out my cheese when baking for better precision. Cup measurements can vary depending on the size of the grating holes.

SHRIMP TOASTS

Who you call'n shrimp?! These buns are dim sum and then some. They're also a fun way to bring some of that "surf" to that "turf." ▪ **MAKES AT LEAST 8 TOASTS**

1 Combine the shrimp, celery, water chestnuts, onion, kimchi, parsley, mayo, egg, sesame oil, salt, and pepper in a food processor and pulse until the mixture resembles a spread but still has a slightly textured consistency. Transfer the spread to a bowl and fold in the sesame seeds and panko.

2 Using a 4-inch ring mold, trim the bread slices into rounds and lightly toast in a toaster or oven.

3 Preheat a cast-iron skillet over medium heat, with 2 tablespoons of olive oil. Using a rubber spatula, spread an even layer of shrimp puree on both sides of a round of toast, then cook until golden brown, 2 to 3 minutes per side. Cook as many at a time as your pan will allow. Add more olive oil as needed. Season with a pinch of salt to finish.

1 pound shrimp, peeled and deveined

2 stalks celery, roughly chopped

½ cup water chestnuts, drained

½ yellow onion, roughly chopped

¼ cup kimchi, drained

1 tablespoon roughly chopped fresh parsley

2 tablespoons homemade mayonnaise (page 166)

1 egg

1 teaspoon sesame oil

1 teaspoon kosher salt, plus more for seasoning

1 teaspoon black pepper

2 tablespoons sesame seeds

¼ cup panko bread crumbs

8 slices potato bread

Extra-virgin olive oil, for panfrying

KALAMATA oLIVE/ONIoN CONFIT AND CHERRY CAKES

Spoiler alert: If you are one of those people who hate the word "moist," read no further. This savory cake is M-O-I-S-T . . . also fluffy. You don't have to be a master baker to get this cake off. The secret to its savory success is in the onion confit, which not only imparts flavor, but also moisty-moistness. ▪ **MAKES 4 CAKES**

1 Make the onion confit: Preheat the oven to 350°F. In a small baking dish, combine the onion and olive oil. Make sure the onions are fully submerged. Bake for 45 minutes. Transfer the onions and olive oil to a blender, puree, and allow to cool. Measure out 1 cup of the puree and reserve the rest for another use.

2 Make the savory cakes: Reduce the oven temperature to 350°F. Grease four 5-inch springform pans.

3 Whisk together the eggs and sugar in a bowl until blended and light in color. Add the buttermilk and onion confit puree and mix until combined.

4 In another bowl, combine the all-purpose flour, almond flour, baking soda, baking powder, and salt. Add the flour mixture to the wet mixture and whisk until combined. Fold in the cherries and olives.

5 Fill the springform pans a little over halfway with batter, place on a baking sheet, and put in the oven. Bake until a toothpick inserted into the center of one cake comes out clean, 35 to 40 minutes. Allow the cakes to cool for 10 minutes in the pan before removing. Finish cooling the cakes on a baking rack.

- 2 small yellow onions, thinly sliced
- 1 cup extra-virgin olive oil
- 3 eggs
- ⅓ cup sugar
- 1¾ cups buttermilk
- 2 cups all-purpose flour
- ¼ cup almond flour
- 1 teaspoon baking soda
- ½ teaspoon baking powder
- 1 teaspoon kosher salt
- ½ cup dried cherries
- ¼ cup Kalamata olives, drained and halved

PINEAPPLE UPSIDE-DOWN CAKES

This cake can always turn my frown upside down. Throw in some crispy Spam and a juicy burger, and I'm sunning on the beaches of my own Hawaiian fantasy. Clothing optional. ▪ **MAKES 4 CAKES**

1 Preheat the oven to 350°F. Grease 4 molds of a hamburger bun tin with the ½ tablespoon butter. Lightly dust each greased mold with a sprinkle of brown sugar, and place a pineapple ring in the middle of each cup.

2 Beat the 10 tablespoons of butter in a bowl until fluffy. Add the light brown sugar and granulated sugar and continue to mix until combined. Add the egg yolks, one at a time, followed by the vanilla, orange zest, cardamom, and milk. Mix until combined.

3 In another bowl, combine the flour, baking powder, and salt. Transfer the flour mixture to the wet ingredients and whisk in by hand, until smooth.

4 Fill the greased bun molds with batter to the top, and bake until the top of each has some color and a toothpick inserted in the center comes out clean, 30 to 35 minutes. Let the cakes cool for 30 minutes. Remove them from the tin by carefully inverting the entire tray upside down. They should slide right out. Place a cherry in the center of each cake before serving.

10 tablespoons butter, plus
  ½ tablespoon for greasing

½ cup packed light brown sugar,
  plus 2 teaspoons for dusting the
  baking tin

4 pineapple rings, drained on
  paper towels

½ cup granulated sugar

5 egg yolks

1 tablespoon vanilla extract

½ teaspoon grated orange zest

½ teaspoon ground cardamom

⅓ cup whole milk

1⅓ cups all-purpose flour

1 teaspoon baking powder

1 teaspoon kosher salt

4 Maraschino cherries

YorKsHIre PUDDING

I like to think of these pastries as a warm hug for my hot beef. To ensure greater pudding puff, make sure your batter is nice and cold before it hits those hot tins. ▪ **MAKES 6 SERVINGS**

1 Whisk together the whole eggs, egg yolk, buttermilk, flour, and salt in a bowl until just combined. Allow the batter to rest for at least 1 hour in the refrigerator.

2 Preheat the oven to 450°F. Grease all 6 cups of a hamburger bun tin (a muffin tin will also work but will yield smaller puddings that will cook faster) with a heaping teaspoon of fat per cup. When the oven gets to temp, place the tin in the oven for about 10 minutes to melt the fat and get the tin sizzling hot

3 Divide the batter evenly among the cups so that they're about halfway filled. Bake until fully risen and golden brown, about 12 minutes. These guys are best served fresh out of the oven.

2 large eggs, beaten
1 egg yolk
¾ cup cold buttermilk
¾ cup all-purpose flour
1 teaspoon kosher salt
½ cup beef leaf, lard, bacon grease, or butter

ROOT VEGETABLE LATKES

These are some hot buns, if I do say so myself, but they can also be used as a crunchy burger filler like in the Slumberjack (page 53). If you want straight-up potato, keep the total amount of shredded root vegetables the same (4½ cups), just change the vegetable game. ▪ **MAKES 8 TO 12 LATKES**

1 In a deep fryer or a deep heavy-bottomed pan with at least 2 inches of oil, preheat your fry oil to 325°F. Preheat the oven to 200°F.

2 Combine the onion, potato, beet, turnip, celery root, eggs, matzoh meal, cornstarch, mustard, and a few pinches each of salt and pepper in a large bowl and mix until fully incorporated. Use a ¼-cup measure to scoop out portions. Shape each portion into roughly shaped patties—stray strands of shredded vegetables are totally OK. They'll crisp up nicely and add texture.

3 Working in batches, carefully place the patties in the hot oil and fry until golden brown and crispy, 4 to 5 minutes. Depending on the size of your frying vessel, you can probably fry a few at a time. Drain them on paper towels and season with salt. Throw them in the oven to keep warm while you fry the remaining batches.

Canola oil, for deep-frying
1 cup shredded onion
1½ cups shredded russet (baking) potato
1 cup shredded candy cane beet
1 cup shredded turnip or rutabaga
1 cup shredded celery root
3 large eggs, beaten
3 tablespoons matzoh meal
2 teaspoons cornstarch
1 teaspoon Dijon mustard
Kosher salt and black pepper

WHOLE KERNEL CORN/JALAPEÑO BATTER

I once dreamed of starting a Led Zeppelin corn dog cover band. . . . For better or worse, Dazed and Cornfused was as far as I got. From corn dogs to Horn Dogs (page 28), this crispy corn batter is my preferred method for eating meat on a stick. ▪ **MAKES 8 TO 12 CORN DOGS OR 4 HORN DOGS (WITH BATTER LEFT OVER FOR ANOTHER USE)**

1 In a deep fryer or a deep heavy-bottomed pan with at least 2 inches of oil, preheat your fry oil to 375°F.

2 Combine the cornmeal, flour, baking powder, salt, black pepper, cayenne, buttermilk, water, honey, eggs, corn, and jalapeño in a medium bowl and stir until incorporated.

3 To assemble the Horn Dog (page 28), start by sliding a smash-cooked PornBurger down a skewer, followed by a slice of pork belly, followed by a slice of pickled hot dog—then finally ONE MORE smash-cooked beef burger. Dip the skewer into the batter using a pair of tongs and fry in the hot oil until golden brown, 4 to 5 minutes. Drain on paper towels and finish with a healthy dribble of clover honey.

Canola oil, for deep-frying
2 cups yellow cornmeal
¾ cup all-purpose flour
4 teaspoons baking powder
½ teaspoon kosher salt
¼ teaspoon black pepper
⅛ teaspoon cayenne pepper
1¼ cups buttermilk
½ cup water
¼ cup clover honey
2 eggs, beaten
Kernels from 2 ears of corn
1 jalapeño, diced

HORN DOG ASSEMBLY (MAKES 4):
8 smash-cooked PornBurgers (page 91)
4 corn dog or wooden skewers
4 slices of slow-roasted pork belly, seared
4 slices of pickled hot dog

SIDEKICKS

GUACAMOLE BONBONS

From one great sidekick to another: "Holy fucking guacamole, Batman!" Why dip chips when you can "chip" dips?! Bite-size blasts of creamy guacamole in a crunchy, corn chip casing. Stoners rejoice. ▪ **MAKES 4 SERVINGS**

1 Make the guacamole bonbons: Mash the avocados in a bowl, making sure to leave some chunks. Use a rubber spatula to fold in the cilantro, onion, tomato, jalapeño, lime juice, salt, and pepper.

2 Spoon the guacamole into a silicone hemisphere mold, wrap with plastic wrap, and freeze for at least 1 hour. If you don't have a silicone mold, use a tablespoon to scoop the guacamole into balls onto a baking sheet lined with wax paper, wrap in plastic wrap, and freeze.

3 Set up the coating: Mix the ground tortilla chips, cornmeal, chili powder, garlic powder, onion powder, and cumin in a bowl. Crack the eggs into another bowl and beat.

4 In a deep fryer or a deep heavy-bottomed pan with at least 2 inches of oil, preheat your fry oil to 375°F.

5 Dredge the frozen guacamole bites in the egg and then in the tortilla chip mixture. Lower into the hot oil using a skimmer or heat-resistant slotted spoon, and fry until browned and crispy, about 3 minutes. Drain well on paper towels and season with salt, and an optional squeeze of lime juice and a crumble of cotija cheese. Serve hot.

GUACAMOLE BONBONS:
 3 avocados, pitted and peeled
 3 tablespoons fresh cilantro, chopped
 ½ red onion, diced
 1 Roma (plum) tomato, diced
 1 jalapeño, minced
 1½ limes, juiced
 1 teaspoon kosher salt
 ½ teaspoon black pepper

BONBON COATING:
 ½ cup ground tortilla chips
 ¼ cup yellow cornmeal
 1 teaspoon chili powder
 1 teaspoon garlic powder
 1 teaspoon onion powder
 ½ teaspoon ground cumin
 2 eggs

 Canola oil, for deep-frying
 Kosher salt
 Limes, for squeezing (optional)
 Crumbled cotija cheese (optional)

CRISPY GNOCCHI TOTS

Tit for tots, these crispy pillows of potato and Parmesan goodness are my favorite way to burger. (Yes, "burgering" is now a verb.) I usually make double batches of this sidekick so that I can freeze extra portions and drop it like it's tot when needed on the fly. ▪ **MAKES 4 SERVINGS**

1 Combine the potatoes and salted cold water to cover in a saucepan and bring to boil. Boil the potatoes until fork-tender, 45 minutes to 1 hour. Cut the potatoes into quarters and run through a ricer or a fine-mesh sieve into a bowl. Allow the potatoes to cool for about 1 hour.

2 Stir the cornstarch, flour, Parmesan, 1 teaspoon salt, Worcestershire powder, and egg into the riced potatoes. Gently knead until a dough forms, then allow to rest for 30 minutes.

3 Divide the dough into quarters and roll each portion out into a rope 1 inch thick. Cut cross-wise into gnocchi-size pieces about ½ inch wide.

4 Set up a large bowl of ice and water. Bring a large pot of salted water to a boil. Working in batches, cook the gnocchi in the boiling water until they float from the bottom to the top, 40 to 60 seconds. Scoop the cooked gnocchi into the ice bath to cool, then drain on paper towels. Repeat until all the gnocchi have been cooked.

5 In a deep fryer or a deep heavy-bottomed pan with at least 2 inches of oil, preheat your fry oil to 375°F.

6 Fry the gnocchi until golden brown, about 2 to 3 minutes, removing them with a skimmer or slotted spoon. Drain the crispy tots on paper towels and season with salt. Extra portions can be frozen, and fried (right out of the freezer) as needed. Garnish with Parmesan and serve with burger sauce for next-level gluttony.

2 large russet (baking) potatoes, scrubbed

Kosher salt

¼ cup cornstarch

6 tablespoons all-purpose flour

¾ cup freshly grated Parmesan, plus more for garnish

1 tablespoon Worcestershire powder

1 extra-large egg, beaten (I use a duck egg when I can find one)

Canola oil, for deep-frying

PornBurger Smoky Burger Sauce (page 166), for serving

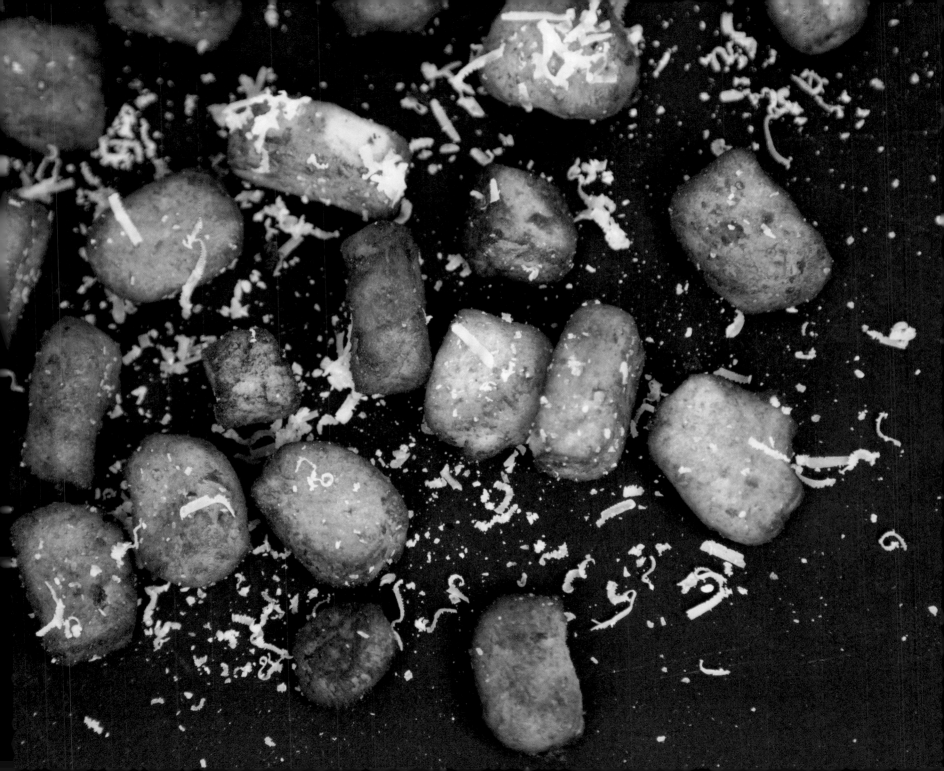

BEEF LEAF FRIES WITH GREMOLATA

The slogan for these fries is "Just suet." Leaf fat is considered the highest grade of fat (or suet) in both bovine and swine alike, and it resides around the animal's kidneys and loin. Mild in flavor, rendered beef leaf (or tallow) has a high smoking point, which makes it great for frying. It's also loaded with naturally occurring B6, B12, K2, selenium, iron, phosphorus, potassium, and riboflavin, which makes beef leaf a considerably healthier alternative to vegetable oils and vegetable shortenings. Red Apron is my go-to source for beef leaf in DC; otherwise you can ask your local butcher for beef leaf tallow. Duck fat also makes for a perfectly awesome alternative. ▪ MAKES 4 TO 6 SERVINGS

1 Make the beef leaf fries: Combine the potatoes with enough cold water to cover in a large pot. Add the salt and vinegar and bring to a boil over high heat. Cook the potatoes until-fork tender, about 15 minutes. Drain and allow the potatoes to cool to room temperature.

2 Preheat the beef leaf to 300°F in a large cast-iron skillet or deep fryer.

3 Add the fries and cook, stirring occasionally, until they begin to turn color, about 5 minutes. Drain and allow to cool. (At this point, you can also freeze the fries for later use. In fact, if you have the time, I'd recommend freezing before refrying for a better crisp factor.)

4 Meanwhile, make the gremolata: Combine the garlic, parsley, Parmesan, and lemon zest in a small bowl.

5 Crank the fat up to 375°F. Add the once-cooked potatoes and fry until nice and crispy and golden brown, 3 to 5 minutes. Drain, season with salt, and toss with gremolata.

BEEF LEAF FRIES:

- 8 small russet (baking) potatoes, skin on, cut into ¼ x ¼-inch sticks for French fries or quartered into wedges for home fries
- 2 tablespoons kosher salt, plus more for seasoning
- Splash of vinegar
- Rendered beef leaf tallow, for deep-frying

GREMOLATA:

- 1 tablespoon minced garlic
- 1 tablespoon chopped fresh parsley
- 1 tablespoon grated Parmesan cheese
- Grated zest of 1 lemon

BLACK GARLIC FRIES WITH BONE MARROW POUTINE

Cooking bone marrow sounds like a potentially daunting task, but, honestly, it doesn't get any easier. ▪ **MAKES 4 TO 6 SERVINGS**

1 Roast the bone marrow: Preheat the oven to 450°F. Place the bones, marrow side up, in a cast-iron or ovenproof skillet and sprinkle with salt and pepper. Roast until the marrow softens and the top begins to bubble, 15 to 20 minutes.

2 Allow the bones to cool before extracting the marrow with a knife. The marrow, about 96 percent fat, is being used as a butter substitute in the poutine sauce and needs to be smooth. So puree the marrow with an immersion blender or in a food processor until smooth.

3 Preheat the oven to 200°F.

4 Make the poutine sauce: In the same pan used to roast the marrow bones, melt the butter and marrow together over low heat. Once the butter has melted, stir in the flour to make a roux. Stir the mixture and cook until smooth and beginning to brown, 2 to 3 minutes. Add the shallot and garlic and continue to cook for another minute. Stir in the HP Sauce and veal stock. Bring to a gentle simmer and cook until the gravy thickens, about 10 minutes. If the gravy becomes too thick, you can always add more stock. Remove from the heat, strain, and keep warm until ready to serve.

5 Make the black garlic fries: Make a fresh batch of beef leaf fries and toss with 1 tablespoon parsley and half of the black garlic. Plate as individual portions or on a burger. Finally, hit those fries with a handful of cheese curds, the remaining parsley and black garlic, and an unhealthy drizzle of warm poutine gravy. Leftover gravy can be stored in the refrigerator for up to 3 days.

PRO TIP: If you're squeamish about blood in your marrow, soak the bones in cold water, salted like the sea, for 12 to 16 hours. Change out the water every 4 hours or so. Pat dry with a paper towel to absorb any remaining blood before roasting.

ROASTED BONE MARROW:

2 to 2½ pounds beef (veal if available) marrow bones, sliced in half lengthwise (ask your butcher to prepare this way)

Kosher salt and black pepper

BONE MARROW POUTINE SAUCE:

About 4 tablespoons roasted bone marrow (the amount of marrow extracted per bone will vary, so make sure to measure)

3 tablespoons butter

¼ cup all-purpose flour

1 shallot, minced

1 clove garlic, minced

1 tablespoon HP Sauce

3½ cups veal stock

Kosher salt and black pepper

BLACK GARLIC FRIES:

1 batch fresh or frozen Beef Leaf Fries (page 263)

2 tablespoons chopped fresh parsley

1 bulb black garlic, diced

2 cups cheddar cheese curds

CHICKEN-FRIED POPCORN SWEETBREADS

OK, OK, I should probably come clean. Nowhere in this recipe is there actually chicken, popcorn, OR bread. So what gives? Well, "deep-fried veal thymus gland" just doesn't have the same ring to it. Sweetbreads are what I categorize as "gateway offal." Not only do they have a cool contradictory nickname—like calling a large man "Tiny"—they've personally opened up a whole universe of innard awesomeness and exploration. In this recipe, we fry them like chicken (duh), rendering crispy kernels of Southern-fried goodness on the outside and creamy morsels of decadence on the inside. Be warned: Overindulging is inevitable. Resulting symptoms are: euphoria, bliss, a blinding erection (male and/or female), and the occasional bouts of gout. Who's with me?! • **MAKES 4 SERVINGS**

1 Soak the sweetbreads in 2 cups of the buttermilk for at least 4 hours. This will tame some of those off(al) flavors. Drain and discard the buttermilk.

2 Combine the veal stock, bay leaf, garlic, onion, lemon, thyme, and parsley in a medium pot and bring to a boil. Rinse the sweetbreads with cold water and add them to the bouillon. Gently simmer until slightly firm but with some bounce when you touch them, about 7 minutes. Drain and remove the sweetbreads from the court bouillon, then allow them to cool on a cutting board.

3 In a deep fryer or a deep heavy-bottomed pan with at least 2 inches of oil, preheat your fry oil to 300°F.

4 Using a paring knife and your fingers, remove the outer membrane and tissue from the sweetbreads so that they become bite-size.

1 pound fresh veal sweetbreads

4 cups buttermilk

3 cups veal or chicken stock

1 bay leaf

2 cloves garlic, smashed

1 small onion, quartered

1 lemon, quartered

6 sprigs thyme

6 sprigs parsley

Canola or peanut oil, for deep-frying

½ cup Fried Chicken Seasoning (page 147)

RECIPE CONTINUES ▶▶

5 Liberally season the sweetbreads with some of the fried chicken seasoning. Whisk together the flour, 2 tablespoons of the fried chicken seasoning, and a dribble of the remaining 2 cups buttermilk. Pour the remaining buttermilk and a pinch of salt into another bowl. Dredge all of the sweetbreads in the flour first, dusting off the excess. Next, submerge each nugget in the buttermilk, again letting the excess drip off, and then toss them back in the flour mixture to fully coat. Once fully battered, allow the sweetbreads to rest for 5 minutes.

6 When your oil is at temperature, fry the sweetbreads until golden brown and crispy, about 5 minutes. Drain, season with salt, and serve warm with the aioli or green goddess dressing for dipping.

2 cups all-purpose flour

Kosher salt

Black Garlic Aioli (page 168) or Tarragon Green Goddess Dressing (page 170), for serving

PORNBURGER QUICKIE:

UNDER PRESSURE

If you've never cooked with a pressure cooker, the first time can be a little intimidating. I mean, why would anyone want to cook under ALL THAT PRESSURE?! Well for starters, it's easy. It's also the culinary weapon of choice for cutting cook times in half for things like braised meats, broths, legumes, and other traditionally slow-cooked foods. Pressure be praised!

Historically, pressure cookers have been around since the late 1600s, but they dropped out of fashion when frozen foods and the microwave revolution came into vogue. That said, modernist chefs are once again dusting them off the shelves of wrinkled records to utilize their miraculous powers for culinary good, and you should too. (That's what we call peer pressure.)

CHICKEN-FRIED PIG EARS

What did Van Gogh say to his pet pig?

"Can you ear me now?"

I know, I know. . . . These jokes are getting seriously ear-ritating. I'm done. These chicken-fried pig ears add a nice porky crunch to just about any stack you want to hack, but they also make for a lovely stand-alone snack. I often serve them with my Pineapple Gastrique (page 188) or my Mustard Green Aioli (page 168), and ALWAYS with a cold beer. To cut down on braising time (by half), I throw them in a pressure cooker. ▪ **MAKES ENOUGH FOR 4 BURGERS**

1 Braise the pig ears: Place the pig ears in a large pot of cold water, bring to a boil, and cook for a few minutes. Use tongs to remove the ears and dump the water. This will help remove some of the impurities.

2 Return the ears to the same pot and add the onion, celery, carrots, garlic, bay leaf, thyme, parsley, peppercorns, and enough water to cover everything. Bring to a gentle simmer over medium heat and cover the pot. Continue to cook the ears for 3 to 4 hours (or half that time if you're using a pressure cooker). They're done when a knife passes through them easily. (Save the braising liquid to use for a pork stock.)

3 Remove the ears and place them on a baking sheet lined with parchment paper. Put another piece of parchment paper over the ears, then another baking sheet on top with weight to add pressure (a heavy pan or a pot filled with water), and let cool. Cut the ears into ¼-inch-thick slices.

4 Fry the pig ears: In a deep fryer or a deep heavy-bottomed pan with at least 2 inches of oil, preheat your fry oil to 350°F.

5 Combine the flour, cornstarch, and fried chicken seasoning in a bowl. Pour the buttermilk into a second bowl. Dredge the slivers of ear in the flour mixture first, then in the buttermilk, and then back into the flour, shaking off the excess. When all the slivers have been dredged, place them in the fryer and cook until golden brown, 2 to 3 minutes. Drain on paper towels, season with the salt, and serve immediately.

BRAISING:
- 2 pig ears
- 1 onion, roughly chopped
- 2 stalks celery, roughly chopped
- 2 large carrots, roughly chopped
- 2 cloves garlic, peeled
- 1 bay leaf
- 6 sprigs thyme
- 6 sprigs parsley
- 10 black peppercorns

FRYING:
- Canola oil, for deep-frying
- 1 cup all-purpose flour
- ½ cup cornstarch
- 1 tablespoon Fried Chicken Seasoning (page 147)
- 1 cup buttermilk
- 2 pinches of kosher salt

SHUT-THE-FUCK-UP PUPPIES (OYSTER AND CRAB HUSH PUPPIES)

There are hush puppies and then there are SHUT-THE-FUCK-UP puppies. What's the difference? Only a whole lotta seafood steez. I may not be super into nutrition, but I'm pretty sure all of that seafood is more than enough to flip the scale toward healthy again . . . am I right? ▪ **MAKES 4 SERVINGS**

1 In a deep fryer or a deep heavy-bottomed pan with at least 2 inches of oil, preheat your fry oil to 325°F.

2 Combine the cornmeal, flour, baking powder, sugar, salt, black pepper, garlic powder, cayenne, buttermilk, sour cream, corn, green onions, jalapeño, parsley, oysters, and crab in a medium bowl and carefully mix until combined.

3 When your oil is up to temp, use a tablespoon to scoop the batter and carefully drop it in the oil. Fry until golden brown and cooked through, about 5 minutes. Drain the puppies on paper towels and season them with salt and Old Bay. Garnish with green onions and serve warm. I like to accompany them with kimchi ketchup.

Canola oil, for deep-frying
2 cups yellow cornmeal
1 cup all-purpose flour
4 teaspoons baking powder
4 teaspoons sugar
2 teaspoons kosher salt
1 teaspoon black pepper
1 teaspoon garlic powder
½ teaspoon cayenne pepper
1 cup buttermilk
½ cup sour cream
Kernels from 1 ear of corn
⅓ cup chopped green onions, plus more for garnish
1 jalapeño, minced
1 tablespoon fresh parsley
1 cup shucked oysters, roughly chopped into big chunks
1 cup cooked crabmeat
Kosher salt and Old Bay seasoning
Kimchi Ketchup (page 174), for serving

KIMCHI TEMPURA

I think of this sidekick as the fried pickle's sexier older sister. (And you thought the fried pickle was an only child.) This dish can easily stand on its own two legs, but it also makes for a great burger wingman (see the So Kalbi Maybe, page 54). ▪ **MAKES 4 SERVINGS**

1 In a deep fryer or a deep heavy-bottomed pan with at least 2 inches of oil , preheat your fry oil to 350°F.

2 Combine the seltzer, flour, cornstarch, and egg in a small bowl and whisk together. (This tempura batter is extremely thin and works well with kimchi, but if you want to use it to fry something else, thicken the batter by cutting back on the amount of seltzer.)

3 Dredge the kimchi in the batter and carefully drop into the oil. Fry until crispy, 3 to 5 minutes. Drain the tempura on paper towels and season with a light dusting of smoked paprika.

Canola oil, for deep-frying
1 cup cold seltzer water
½ cup all-purpose flour
½ cup cornstarch
1 egg, whisked
2 cups kimchi (depending on what form it comes in, you might want to chiffonade so that it is thinly sliced)
A few pinches of smoked sweet paprika

PORN STARS IRL

HONEYCOMB GROCER, DC

1309 5TH STREET NE, WASHINGTON, DC 20002

UNIONMARKETDC.COM

For a city whose reputation is built on being hyper international, sourcing Asian ingredients in Washington, DC, has historically been an exercise in frustration of "blue ball" proportions. Enter culinary dragon Erik Bruner-Yang (of Toki Underground and Maketto) and his assembled dynamic duo, Isaiah Billington and Sarah Conezio (previously of Woodberry Kitchen). With their energies combined, they have harnessed the power of locally sourced ingredients and elevated them to a house-made selection of Asian awesomeness in a space called Honeycomb. The space is not much bigger than an actual pantry, but it boasts a spectacular array of fermentation from kimchi to hoisin, and even a house-made soy sauce. Not only is Honeycomb the grocery DC needs, it's the grocery our capital deserves.

PRO TIP:

IF YOU'RE IN DC, I HIGHLY RECOMMEND HONEYCOMB'S SEA KRAUT KIMCHI, WHICH IS FERMENTED WITH LOCALLY SOURCED VEGGIES AND CHESAPEAKE OYSTERS.

SHOESTRING ONION RINGS

These fun-ions are thin for the win. Eat them by the fistful or embellish your stacksimus maximus with some added allium crunch. ▪ **MAKES 4 SERVINGS**

1 Soak the onions in the buttermilk for at least 1 hour. Drain and discard the buttermilk.

2 In a deep fryer or a deep heavy-bottomed pan with at least 2 inches of oil, preheat your fry oil to 375°F.

3 Whisk together the flour, cornstarch, salt, black pepper, cayenne, paprika, and garlic powder in a small bowl until combined.

4 When the oil is at temp, dredge the onions in the flour mixture, shaking off the excess, and fry until golden brown and crispy. Drain on paper towels and season with a sprinkle of salt.

2 large onions, cut into ⅛-inch-thick slices
2 cups buttermilk
Vegetable oil, for deep-frying
1½ cups all-purpose flour
¼ cup cornstarch
1 tablespoon kosher salt, plus more for seasoning
2 teaspoons black pepper
¼ teaspoon cayenne pepper
¼ teaspoon sweet paprika
¼ teaspoon garlic powder

WHISTLE WHETTERS

THE LIQUID DIET

It's 5:30 p.m. somewhere and this slutty sipper with a bacon straw is just begging to be slurped down in all of its burger glory. White Castle–infused Bulleit rye, stirred with spicy pickle juice, a splash of tomato water, and a dash of liquid smoke, and rimmed with a burger salt rub, almost makes this elixir a knife-and-forker. And you thought tequila made you rowdy. ▪ **MAKES 6 COCKTAILS**

1 Make the infused rye: Take the warm White Castle patties and stuff them into the iSi cream whipper, along with the rye whiskey. Charge the canister with N$_2$O and shake for a couple of minutes. Charge the canister with another hit of N$_2$O and shake for 1 minute before letting rest for 3 to 5 minutes. Slowly vent the gas before opening the canister and straining the liquid into a cup. Place the infused whiskey in the freezer to cool for about 20 minutes. The goal is for any fats and oils that transferred to the whiskey to solidify. Strain the whiskey through a coffee filter to clarify.

2 Make the tomato water: Puree the tomatoes in a food processor (or juicer if you have one) and strain through a fine-mesh sieve. Pour the tomato juice through a coffee filter to clarify into clear "water." Repeat as many times as needed until all the tomato solids are removed.

3 Make the bacon swizzles: Preheat the oven to 375°F. Line a baking sheet with parchment paper. Grease the metal straws with oil to prevent sticking.

4 Wrap a slice of bacon around each straw so that the bacon is fairly tight and slightly overlapping. Place the bacon-wrapped straws on the baking sheet and bake until the bacon is crispy, 15 to 20 minutes. Once cooked, allow to cool and then carefully slide the bacon off of the metal straws and drain on paper towels.

5 For each cocktail: 2 ounces infused rye, 1 ounce tomato water, 1 ounce pickle juice, and 3 dashes of liquid smoke. Spear a pickle slice, a cocktail onion, and a cherry tomato on each of six toothpicks. Garnish each cocktail with a bacon swizzle and the speared vegetables.

WHITE CASTLE–INFUSED RYE:
- 6 frozen White Castle hamburgers, cooked
- iSi cream whipper
- 1½ cups rye whiskey (preferably Bulleit)

TOMATO WATER:
- 1 pound vine-ripened tomatoes

BACON SWIZZLES:
- 6 metal straws
- Canola oil, for greasing the pan
- 6 slices smoked bacon

ASSEMBLY:
- 6 ounces pickle juice (preferably from spicy pickles)
- Liquid smoke
- 6 dill pickle slices
- 6 pickled cocktail onions
- 6 cherry tomatoes
- McCormick Burger Seasoning*

* Available in the spice section of your grocery store or online

MALTED UNDERBERG MILKSHAKE

Quite possibly the lamest thing I ever got in trouble for when growing up was stealing some Bailey's Irish Cream from my parents' liquor cabinet in order to have an "adult" milkshake in the parking lot before school. Not only was the experience buzz free, it also left me with a lingering dairy-ache, and a lot of "me" time after my parents passed punishment. This boozy milkshake harnesses the power of actual adulthood, to deliver a mysterious meld of flavor intrigue AND actual digestive powers to boot. #TheMoreYouKnow. ▪ **MAKES 1 MILKSHAKE**

Combine 1 bottle of the bitters, the malted milk powder, milk, and ice cream in a blender (or use an immersion blender). Blend the ingredients until combined and pour into a glass. I use the second bottle of the bitters as a floater that I can stir in smugly.

Two 20ml bottles Underberg* bitters

4 teaspoons malted milk powder

¼ cup whole milk

2½ cups vanilla ice cream

* Available from the liquor store, in the bitters section, or online

PORNBURGER QUICKIE:

UNDER-WHAT?!

Burger comas, say *auf Wiedersehen*. Hailing from Germany, Underberg is a cure-all for overindulgence. But seriously, what is it? As the bottle reads, "Underberg is an herb bitters taken for digestion, it is not a beverage. Not to be sipped, but taken all at once and quickly because of its aromatic and strong taste." These single-serving salvos (made with a secret list of herbs from more than forty-three countries) pack just the punch to put some pep back in your step.

'ROUND MIDNIGHT

A peanut butter bacon milkshake with salted bacon dulce de leche and bourbon. Whatever you do, do not, <u>under any circumstance</u>, make this milkshake. There can be no turning back. ▪ **MAKES 1 MILKSHAKE**

Combine the ice cream and bourbon in a blender and blend until combined. If it's too thick (as if), you can add a little milk or more bourbon to taste. Drizzle a milkshake glass with the dulce de leche and then pour in the shake. Garnish with more dulce de leche and candied bacon bits.

- 2½ cups **Peanut Butter Bacon Ice Cream** (recipe follows)
- ¼ cup **bourbon**
- 1 tablespoon **Sous-Vide Bacon Dulce de Leche** (recipe follows)
- **Caramel bacon**, for garnish (optional; from the dulce de leche)

PEANUT BUTTER BACON ICE CREAM

MAKES ABOUT 1 QUART

1 Preheat the oven to 350°F.

2 Line up the bacon on a baking sheet (since you also need 3 slices for the dulce de leche, below, add those slices to the baking sheet too). Lightly sprinkle the brown sugar evenly over 9 of the slices and bake until crispy, 15 to 20 minutes. Drain the bacon on a wire rack. (Set the 3 uncoated slices aside for the dulce de leche.)

3 Combine the sugar-coated cooked bacon, the buttermilk, cream, sugar, vanilla, and salt in a medium pot and bring to a simmer over low heat, stirring occasionally to prevent sticking as well as to dissolve the sugar. As soon as the mixture starts to simmer, remove from the heat. Allow this base to cool for at least 1 hour or even overnight in the refrigerator.

- 9 slices **thick-cut bacon**
- A couple of pinches of **light brown sugar**
- 1½ cups **buttermilk**
- 1⅓ cups **heavy (whipping) cream**
- 1½ cups **granulated sugar**
- 1 teaspoon **vanilla extract**
- A pinch of **kosher salt**
- 8 **egg yolks**, beaten
- ½ cup **chunky peanut butter**

RECIPE CONTINUES ▶▶

4 Strain the mixture and discard the bacon. Some bacon fat will have rendered into the cream mixture, but the fat will help impart flavor and additional creaminess. Whisk in the egg yolks and peanut butter.

5 Pour the mixture into an ice cream maker and freeze according to the manufacturer's instructions. Store the ice cream in the freezer to harden it.

SOUS-VIDE BACON DULCE DE LECHE
MAKES ABOUT 2 CUPS

Set your sous-vide water bath to 185°F using your immersion circulator. Pour the condensed milk into a sterilized canning jar and add the bacon. Seal the jar and place it in the water bath so that it's completely submerged. Cover the water bath with foil or a lid to conserve energy. Cook the condensed milk for 15 hours. Remove the bacon and reserve for garnish.

One 14-ounce can condensed milk
3 slices thick-cut bacon, crisp-cooked

COCONUT HORCHATA FROSTEEZES

With this styling summer steez, brain freeze is inevitable. It can't be helped. Consider it a side effect of having your mind blown. Is this a super-traditional take on Mexican horchata? Not even close. But that ship sailed a long time ago. Despite the addition of rum, this isn't a super-boozy drink. Should your booze lust demand a quenching of a higher calling, by all means, top her off with an additional floater of spiced rum. ▪ **MAKES 6 TO 8 SERVINGS (2 QUARTS)**

1 Pour 3 cans of the coconut milk into a large pot. Add the cinnamon stick and sugar and bring to a gentle simmer over medium-low heat. Stir occasionally to prevent anything from sticking to the bottom. Once the milk begins to simmer, remove from the heat and stir in the remaining coconut milk.

2 In a blender, pulse the rice to get a coarse grind. Be careful not to completely pulverize the rice, as you'll want to strain the rice out later. Add the rice to the pot and allow it to soak covered on your counter for at least 3 hours or overnight. Strain the liquid through a fine-mesh sieve into a plastic quart container. Stir in the cinnamon and rum and freeze.

3 Once the horchata is almost completely frozen, after 60 to 90 minutes, blend until smooth and creamy and serve cold.

Four 14-ounce cans coconut milk
1 stick cinnamon
1 cup plus 3 tablespoons sugar
1 cup long-grain white rice
2 teaspoons ground cinnamon
4 ounces spiced rum (I find Flor de Caña 7-year aged rum is a good fit)

BURNT CREAMSICLE

This smoky-citrus cream dream is essentially all of my childhood favorites, filtered through my adult tendencies. Serve these chill pills poolside with a grilled burger and a Speedo to become a lifelong, card-carrying member of the high-five club. ▪ **MAKES 4 TO 6 SERVINGS**

1 Make the orange margarita granita: Combine the sugar and water in a saucepan and bring to a simmer, stirring until all of the sugar has dissolved. Remove from the heat and add the orange zest, orange juice, mezcal, and agave nectar. Freeze for at least 9 hours in a sealable container and use a fork to stir and break it up every few hours.

2 Make the cold-smoked condensed milk: Pour the condensed milk into another sealable container. Using a smoking gun, fill the container with applewood smoke before sealing. Allow the smoke to sit in the container for 10 to 15 minutes. Release the smoke and stir. If you desire more of a smoky flavor, simply seal with smoke for an additional 5 minutes.

3 If desired, make the brûléed orange garnish: Dip the frozen orange slices in superfine sugar. Use a brulée torch to caramelize the sugar.

4 To assemble the drinks, use a fork to fill coupe glasses (or weapon of choice) with orange margarita granita. Drizzle the smoked sweetened condensed milk over the granita with a spoon, and stir to combine. Garnish with a brûléed orange wedge.

ORANGE MARGARITA GRANITA:
- 1 cup sugar
- 1 cup water
- Grated zest of 1 orange
- 1⅔ cups fresh orange juice (about 4 large oranges)
- 5 tablespoons smoky mezcal
- 2 tablespoons agave nectar

COLD-SMOKED CONDENSED MILK:
- One 14-ounce can condensed milk
- Smoking gun
- Applewood smoking chips

BRÛLÉED ORANGE GARNISH (OPTIONAL):
- 1 orange, cut into thin wedges and frozen
- ¼ cup superfine sugar
- Brûlée torch

Note: Page references in *italics* indicate recipe photographs.

...W-W-WHAT ARE YOU...

THIS CURSE IS MY BURDEN TO BEAR!!